LET PRAYER CHANGE YOUR LIFE

LET PRAYER CHANGE YOUR LIFE

BECKY TIRABASSI

BECKY
TIRABASSI
change your life®

Published by Becky Tirabassi Change Your Life®, Inc.
Box 9672, Newport Beach, Ca. 92660

Library of Congress Cataloging-in-Publication Data
Tirabassi, Becky, 1954—
        Let Prayer Change Your Life, Becky Tirabassi
ISBN 0-7852-7721-8 (pbk.)
ISBN 0-7852-6885-5 (revised pbk.)
ISBN 0-9677198-5-2 (current edition)
ISBN 978-0-9677198-5-6(current edition)
Printed in the United States of America

Letter from Becky...
February 2007

Dear Reader:

In February of 1984, I discovered prayer at a youth worker convention, then proceeded (out of character) to make a non-negotiable decision in front of another person to pray for one hour a day for the rest of my life! Quickly realizing that I did not know how to pray, I asked God for a design for prayer that would keep me accountable and organized—and the rest is history! *My Partner Prayer Notebook* was born, my prayer ministry began and over 250,000 men, women and students have used this notebook as their companion in prayer! Most importantly, with great enthusiasm, I continue to teach people of all ages to "pray the write way."

The journey that began over twenty years ago is captured in the following pages of my first book, *Let Prayer Change Your Life* which also includes a fasting addendum (added in the year 2000). *Let Prayer Change Your Life Workbook* is a companion to this book and prayer notebook designed to guide one person—or a small group—to take on the challenges of (1) talking and listening to God for one hour each day, (2) practicing the discipline of regular fasting, and (3) making a commitment to change your world through prayer!

Through this book, I am confident that you will be inspired to discover prayer, decide to pray, and develop a design for prayer that will change your life!

Becky

TABLE OF CONTENTS

Acknowledgment

To Roger, my mentor and best friend.

Thank you for investing
in my life and ministry
for over thirty years!

INTRODUCTION

I am convinced that the practice of prayer in a believer's life is an incredible, virtually untapped power source. Not only am I convinced because of my personal experience, but because the lives of many who have been committed to the discipline of daily prayer, during and before our present day, validate that I am not alone in my discovery!

The following pages of this book, I pray, will serve as inspiration and motivation to each reader to consider the power of prayer through a daily appointment with God as an essential and integral part of every day. Stories, sermon excerpts, prayers, and quotes from powerhouses such as Peter Marshall, George Muller, Andrew Murray, and many others will be a constant source of encouragement and exhortation for us to hold onto God when our resistance gets low and our endurance in prayer wavers.

Upon recognition that prayerlessness was sin in my life, I was deeply touched by God to make a commitment to pray for one hour a day. Over twenty-three years (or over 8400 "hours") later, God has changed my personality and character, increased my faith through unbelievable answers to prayer, called me to accountability in numerous areas, and given me a vivid vision of possibilities for His will in my life. Having been a teenage alcoholic, I know that this disciplined prayer life is a work of the Holy Spirit within me, not a privileged performance that I have perfected.

The unfolding of the discipline of prayer in my life was an unexpected surprise. I'm not the kind of person you would normally find sitting still for one hour, much less quietly praying for that amount of time. But because of prayer, I've spent over two decades in an incredible journey with God. To help you more clearly understand prayer and its power from the perspective of a Christian woman—not a scholar, not a pastor, not a seminary student—I believe God has given me five parts in which to explain it.

The first part concerns the discovery of prayer. This part discusses what it is and what it isn't. How do you view prayer? Do you see prayer as a believer's power source or a source of boredom? From the beginning of this book, you will be challenged to change!

Over twenty-three years ago I was at a convention workshop where many speakers were talking about prayer. Had I known the convention would focus on the discipline of prayer, I probably wouldn't have been motivated to attend. Prayer was never a big interest to me as a young Christian, yet when I heard Samuel Chadwick's quote, "Prayerlessness in the life of a believer is sin," I had to take that statement to heart. I had to say, "Either I believe this as truth, or I don't believe it."

What do you believe about prayer?

The second part focuses on what happens when prayer moves from a decision to a discipline. *Discipline* is a serious word much like *prayer*. It means work. It requires a personal cost. My particular personality avoided the cost of discipline before I began a lifestyle of prayer.

Yet, when I was convinced (and convicted) that prayerlessness in my life was sin, I was forced to make a decision. If Jesus Christ was the priority in my life that I told others that He was, then how could I spend so little time with Him on a daily basis?

You make time for those you love. You make time for what

you consider a priority. Think over your last day...your last week . . . your last month. How and with whom did you spend the majority of your time? When I honestly reflected on those questions, I had to stand back and say, "My life is too busy for God!"

At that juncture, I made a non-negotiable decision to pray for one hour a day for the rest of my life. That may sound pious. That may sound spiritual. It was neither. I felt a great need to know God and love God like I had when I first met Him. I was exuberant when I first met Christ. I was dramatically changed! I was enthralled by Him! I was excited to know Him better! I loved talking and listening to God! Then why as an older Christian did I consider spending time with Him a duty or burdensome discipline?

My decision to pray one hour a day took me knee deep into discipline. In fact, on one afternoon in February of 1984, this sanguine, Type "A", young, busy, youth worker, wife and mother decided to pray for one hour a day for the rest of her life.

When I began to pray daily, my priorities changed. It never failed—every day I would meet with God and He would filter through my "to do" list, which at the time included a few hours of watching soap operas and at least an hour of chatting on the phone. I even found an extra twenty minutes in my day by simply adding up all the time I stood in front of the refrigerator wondering what was in there to eat! My time became very important to me because, all of a sudden, I felt it was very important to God.

Psalm 90:12 says, "Teach us to number our days aright, that we may gain a heart of wisdom." It didn't take long before I realized, "Oh, my goodness, Becky, you're wasting so much time that could be spent on making a difference for the kingdom of God."

My perspective of God changed.

He was no longer too small.

Too strict.
Or too far away.
He was near.
He was always with me.
He was powerful.
He was the Creator of the world.
He was my Creator.

Somehow in my fast-paced, busy little Christian life I rarely stopped and said, "You are God. Show me the way to go. You've already planned it. I want to know." No, I hustled and bustled through each day and then figured out at the end of the day (after I had "crashed and burned" a few times) that I would have been better off to consult Him earlier in the day.

Not that I didn't know God. Not that I couldn't say that I loved God. But in my daily hour of prayer, I was truly falling in love with Him as a person, not as a wizard of Oz machine that pumps smoke and firmly says, "No!"

My personality also changed as I spent more time in prayer. How can you spend time with someone and not be influenced by that person's character? I could spend one week with students and walk away saying, "Like, dude, what's happening? Totally, I mean . . ." (It is almost impossible not to talk like those you spend much time around.)

I don't believe you can daily spend time with God and not experience a change in your character or personality. It is inevitable. And so it was with me. With quietness came reflection and conviction. It was amazing how many personality flaws came to the surface, how many things I had been holding inside became my topic of conversations with God.

Yes, I was the child of an alcoholic. Yes, I was an alcoholic myself. Those two characteristics alone create enough reason for psychologists to spend years counseling someone. Yet, an hour a day with God began to unravel, unfold, reveal, and heal the tangled mess that was within me in a gentle, positive, re-newing way.

Then my possibilities changed. I was no longer destined to live in a two-mile radius. Hopes and dreams, ideas and goals, plans and problems bombarded me so quickly that I had to do something about them. God was giving me ideas to change the world, my home, my church, and myself.

You can have this experience! The person God created you to be can be unleashed if you'll just spend time with Him. In the school of prayer, you will get your marching orders! Per-haps it is time to go back to school, to further your education for where He wants to take you next? It is never too late to start clinging to God on a daily basis, to talk to Him and listen to Him daily. Prayer illuminates the difference between know-ing God's will and guessing at it.

The third part of this book is the design for prayer. We'll explore talking to God and recognizing His voice. I love to call this section, "one Christian's secret to a happy hour!"

Hannah Whitall Smith wrote *The Christian's Secret of a Happy Life* over a century ago. She was a woman who read the Bible and believed it. She tried it, tested it, and found it to be true. I contend that you will find your faith will grow immea-surably if you spend time in prayer daily. I have tried it. I have tested it. I have found one hour with the King to be the most important appointment in my day.

Early in my commitment to pray an hour a day, God gave me an idea to develop a resource called *My Partner Prayer Notebook*. It became the tool that kept me organized and ac-countable in my prayer life! It is the practical place where I have recorded my conversations with God every day for over twenty-three years. I even travel with it. I never want to miss what will happen during my hour with God!

The fourth part of this book is an adventure into the delights, desires, and dreams of your heart through prayer. We'll look at six powerful prayer principles as biblical promises in our walk and our relationship with God:

- Receiving prayer
- Believing prayer
- Revealing prayer
- Interceding prayer
- Agreeing prayer
- Persevering prayer

In my life, these principles have led to mounds of miracles, open doors and fulfilled dreams. But they are not just for me! They are available to anyone who will pray!

The last part illustrates how to know God better. What has been the result of praying for over twenty-three years?

I have a much deeper faith.

I've put my hope and trust in His Word.

I've learned to wait more patiently on God.

I've received daily direction and correction.

And I've grown more in love with Him each day.

I urge you to release God's power through a new (or renewed) practice of daily prayer in your life. If, in fact, you are content with your fellowship with the Lord on a daily, perhaps hourly, basis, I trust this book will be refreshing. But if you have a deep hunger for an effective, powerful prayer life, I challenge you to open your heart and mind right now to all of God's Holy Spirit and make a decision to daily spend time talking and listening to Him. If you do, I am confident your life will never be the same because . . .

prayer does,

prayer can, and

prayer will change your life.

PART I
THE DISCOVERY OF PRAYER

WHAT IT IS, WHAT IT ISN'T

Prayer—My Heartthrob?

I've been so dramatically changed and influenced by the discovery of prayer in my life that I couldn't agree more with O. Hallesby's conviction that "prayer is the heartthrob of a believer's life." In fact, when the topic of prayer popped up in a casual dinner conversation with a younger Christian, I automatically asked my favorite mentor-like question, "How's your daily time with God?" Her coy reply was, "Well, I'm not praying as much as I should or I ought . . ."

Though her response didn't seem out of the ordinary, it allowed me to identify the problem of *why* she was struggling with prayer. Her perspective on prayer, as mine had once been, was confused. Prayer had become something she felt she had to do rather than something she wanted, desired, needed, or longed to do.

The "Problem of Prayer"

Prayer is a word that creates a different picture in each of our minds. It seems that most people agree that prayer is a good idea, but it is little practiced at many Christian gatherings, and often when it is the focus of a meeting, the crowds are small or the event is attended mostly by women, rarely by students and men.

Why? Why, in this time of great need for revival, especially in the United States, does a known power source for transformation and change get so little attention?

To answer that question, I needed to look only as far as myself. The reasons that prayer is pushed aside are varied and often based on misconceptions.

Misconception 1: "It's Boring!"

Prayer on the surface may seem boring. Perhaps it's the pure effort involved in true prayer that causes one to quit early without ever seeing the rewarding results of their perseverance? Or perhaps it is boredom that prevails when group prayer sinks to monotone levels? And certainly falling asleep during prayer has been the experience of many a tired believer who reverently closes his eyes and winds up disrupting a prayer meeting or small group due to loud snoring or snorting!

Or the mention of prayer quickly triggers "I've got to get out of here before I'm stuck" reactions in many people—perhaps because most of us are inspired and motivated by the excitement of evangelism, moving preaching, heart-throbbing music and testimony, and yet we possess little knowledge of the power released when one prays.

And wouldn't that just suit the enemy's cause? Disguise prayer as tedious, powerless, for the elderly, or "religious," and you'll keep believers away from it ninety-nine out of one hundred times.

But if prayer was so boring, why didn't the disciples ask Jesus how to perform miracles and healings, instead of asking

Him how to pray (Luke 11)? If prayer was so boring and such a potential time-waster, why did Jesus Himself choose so often to spend time alone in prayer? Who started the rumor that prayer was boring, anyway?

Misconception 2: "Prayer Is for the Pious and the Religious."

Perhaps you've thought, *"I'm not good enough to talk to God. He wouldn't talk to me! He is busy with more important things than my concerns. He doesn't have time for me. Why I'm just. . ."* That misconception holds some truth, but we hold the key that unlocks a shut door.

Yes, it is a biblical statement that God does not listen if we cherish—or hold onto—sin in our hearts (Ps. 66:18), but the Word also states that confession of sin brings His forgiveness (1 John 1:9) and opens the gates of communication with Him. Therefore, an incorrect attitude of false humility suggests we can never be good enough for God to hear—or care for—us; but a broken, contrite, and *humble* heart is the way to the foot of the King's throne—and to the ear of our loving Father!

Misconception 3: "God Doesn't Always Answer Prayer."

Is God able to meet our needs, reverse our circumstances, or change what appears to be impossible? Our perception of God, our belief in *who God says He is* and *what He says about prayer* is crucial to receiving answers to prayer.

A lack of faith—in *anyone*—certainly decreases one's ability to trust in that person; it is no different with God. Those who believe that God cannot or will not answer prayer, owe it to themselves to study the God of the Old and New Testament.

For the Bible speaks boldly of a God
>who performs miracles,
>>brings the dead back to life,
>>>turns the sea into dry land,
>>>>converts sinners instantly into Christ-followers, and
>>>>assigns them as evangelists and apostles!

The God spoken of by the prophets and priests of the Old Testament is all-powerful, all-knowing, and always present; the God of the New Testament manifested in the person of Jesus Christ is personal and powerful, able to forgive the darkest sins and to heal the deadliest diseases. It then becomes a matter of belief that our prayers—as validated in Scripture—will not only will be heard, but will be answered by God! In other words, God *can*, God *will*, and God *does* the impossible when we pray.

What do you believe?

Misconception 4: "My Prayer Has No Power."

In truth, the vast majority of us fall into the classification of ignorance—not rebellion or conscious avoidance, but simply a lack of understanding about the power released when one prays. Ignorance about prayer automatically places many believers into the powerless category of Christian living called "prayerlessness."

Certainly we all enter into a personal relationship with Christ through various circumstances: childhood religion classes, parental spiritual nurturing, during catechism classes, while on a retreat, or through invitations during a crusade or revival meeting. But how many of us were immediately presented with the spiritual discipline of prayer as an on-going, intimate, powerful, exciting, adventurous, and life-directing daily experience, the vital connection we are privileged to have with the God? I think it's safe to assume that only a fortunate few of us were taught and trained to be powerful pray-ers. *If more leaders, mentors, and parents considered prayer as a non-negotiable, two-way conversation with the living, loving God there would be many more of us who loved to pray!*

What is more common? Powerless Christians who find Bible reading and praying too time-consuming for their daily lives, who often think of spiritual disciplines as legalistic, or who are only willing to pray when an urgent need arises and when all else fails.

Results of Prayerlessness

Just as the Public Safety Department of the Automobile Club of Southern California has developed a survey indicating possible problem drinkers—answer one yes and consider it a warning to your problem, two yes answers and you just might be, and three yes answers mean you most likely are a problem drinker—so O. Hallesby has developed a list of the dangerous results of prayerlessness:

- We have more "world" in our thoughts.
- We feel farther away from God.
- We have less "God" talk in our conversations with others.
- Slowly an unwilling or rebellious spirit creeps into our personality.
- Sin doesn't sting as much, because it is less honestly confessed.
- We deal with sin as the world does, by hiding it!

Unfortunately, most of us don't change a lifestyle habit because we've read a list of ways we've neglected our health. Yet I often wonder if I had read a list of the signs of a Christian who neglected prayer and taken it seriously, such as the one above, perhaps I would have been spared great heartache before I reached a dangerous, spiritual drought.

So many of us reach a point where we have no strength, no integrity, no power in our lives—only then do we consider the path of prayer. That, I believe, is where the victory over prayerlessness begins . . . with helplessness.

Andrew Murray in his classic, *The Prayer Life*, devotes numerous chapters to the issue of prayerlessness in a believer's life. A sincere study of his findings, consolations, corrections, and encouragement offers great hope to someone discouraged by self-effort and continuous lack of victory in their pursuit of a true prayer life.

Andrew Murray says,

> "My advice to you is: Give over your restlessness and effort; fall helpless at the feet of the Lord Jesus; He will speak the word, and your soul will 'live.' If you have done this then, second comes the message: "This is but the beginning of everything. It will require deep earnestness, and the exercise of all your power, and a watchfulness of the entire heart—eager to detect the least backsliding. Above all, it will require a *surrender* to a life of self-sacrifice that God really desires to see in us and which He will work out for us."

Bottom line, Murray powerfully suggests,

> "If we recognize, in the first place, that a right relationship to the Lord Jesus, above all else, *includes prayer,* with both the desire and power to pray according to God's will, then we have something which gives us the right to rejoice in Him and to rest in Him (emphasis added)."

Once again, like alcoholics faced with the truth about their problem, we as believers are forced to examine our own prayer lives in the privacy of our hearts. It is only then, with complete dependency upon the Holy Spirit and *His* renewing, revealing power, that we can allow God to speak to us regarding our relationship with Him and the state of our prayer lives, perhaps as we have never before so clearly heard Him.

Is it time for you to . . .

- Let God convince you that prayerlessness in a believer's life is sin?
- Admit your helplessness?
- Confess any known sin and accept God's forgiveness?
- Be encouraged that you are not alone, but you may be a trailblazer for prayer in your home or at your youth group, church, organization, school, city, or state?

If you are ready and willing, then as C. S. Lewis put it, be challenged to change with "a fellow-patient in the same hospital who, having been admitted a little earlier, could give some advice."

CHALLENGED TO CHANGE

The best place for me to start is to simply tell you how it happened in my life. God's power was released immediately following my decision to pray for one hour a day for the rest of my life. That was over twenty-two years ago. Eight-thousand hours later with the Lord, I have great things to report to you.

It was my seventh year as a Christian; even reflecting on how I came to know Christ always elicits a deep emotional reaction within my soul. Becoming a Christian in a dramatic turn of events after struggling for years as an alcoholic student catapulted me into youth ministry. I never really knew any other way to live as a Christian other than in a *daily* relationship, always expecting God to speak to me, love me, and guide me at every turn.

A Fading Faith . . .

But somehow, over time, the zeal and fervor I once couldn't hide if I tried, subtly faded into fond memories without my full awareness. It wasn't until February of 1984 that I recognized a real negative attitude in myself that affected me both outwardly and inwardly.

A list of my character flaws would take the better part of this page, but they weren't my only problem. I was struggling with relationships, weight control, and my thought life. Even the prospects for my future seemed like grains of sand strewn and scattered about randomly rather than a pathway warmly lighted and specifically cut from stone expressly for me to follow.

Integrity, focus, humor, and joy in serving the Lord had almost disappeared, causing me to fit right in with the world.

A Glimpse that Produced Only a Grimace

The "baby Christian" pace of excitement, expectation, and the daily "awe" of God was no longer the rule in my life; it was now the exception.

Somewhere along the way I had fallen prey to the enemy's deceitful voice that said, "Mature Christians don't believe that God does miraculous things in a believer's life for all of life." I was beginning to adopt part of "the honeymoon was over" philosophy.

My once-crucified inherent weaknesses—jealousies, comparisons, compulsiveness, and anger—were resurfacing. Nagging at me, like hunger pains, the least bit of self-evaluation or personal spiritual inventory brought two things to the surface: (1) *what used to be* and (2) *what was no more!*

Upon my conversion to Christ in 1976, my initial need for God was so great that I considered Him my constant companion and friend—sensing His presence with me at all times. In the beginning of our relationship, I would consult Him on the most extraordinary and seemingly impossible opportunities and blindly trust His power to intervene. For instance, in my first month as a believer, I felt that God wanted me to return to my parent's home—to show them my new life in

Christ. So, I simply asked God for a ride from California to Ohio. Daily I prayed that He would help me get home.

A used car salesman had always been friendly toward me, though we had little in common other than our business relationship. After I told him of my conversion to Christ, he looked at me as if I wasn't "all there," perhaps thinking drugs had altered my emotional and mental state. Whereas once I had been a party-going, wild young woman, all I could do now was to enthusiastically talk about my relationship with Jesus.

When I told him that I felt "God wanted me to return to Ohio," he only chuckled. My faith was very childlike at that point in time; therefore, I wasn't embarrassed because I felt God was as real as this man was, and if someone was going to laugh at me, I would prefer it be the used car salesman instead of God. Ironically, within the next few days, this very salesman returned to my desk and said to me, "You won't believe this. I have a friend in Ohio who owns a twenty-nine-foot motor home that has been in storage up in Oakland, California. He has been unable to transport it back to Ohio and he wondered if you would be interested in driving it home to his car dealership."

Well, I looked at my salesman friend and said, "I told you God would find a way!" Immediately, I imagined my bike, furniture, silverware, clothes—everything—loaded into this motor home, saving shipping charges. A day or two later I received a telegram that authorized me to drive this motor home, free of charge, free of fuel charges, all the way back to Ohio. Though it could have seemed coincidental to some, for me, it felt as if my Friend, Jesus, had literally provided a way home for me, knowing that I didn't have any money to do it on my own.

With the same confident assurance that Jesus would show me His will in big decisions, I would inquire of my close Friend about the most minute and seemingly unimportant-to-anyone-else requests, such as what to wear, where to spend my free time, what I should talk to non-Christians about, and which sections I should read in the Bible. My basic question became, "What would You have me do today, Lord?" You see, I had lived in the world so long and made so many decisions based on feelings or on what others did and thought that I became quickly dependent upon God's nudge for every little detail of my life.

And with the same fervency, I was consumed with the Bible. I quickly understood that if I wanted to hear God's voice, I needed to read His Word, the Bible. I read incessantly, diligently searching for His advice on issues such as purity, honesty, and discipline—all areas in which I had struggled for many years. Enthralled with the eye-opening stories of the early disciples in the book of Acts and the principles for daily Christian living as set forth by Jesus, Paul, and John, I took God's Word as literal and powerful and I carried it with me everywhere.

From Burned Out to Turned Around!

Years later, as a youth worker, I mundanely pulled manuals off a shelf, referred to proven ministry methods rather than developed my own, read a bit of my Bible each night in bed (though it would often fall on my face, only to rudely wake me up), prayed occasionally for "a touch from God," and regularly fell asleep during prayer time with my husband.

How in the world did I get from one extreme to the other? I loved Jesus! I loved to talk about Him! I gladly evangelized! Except, except...even that had been conveniently shrugged off over the previous few months. The burning flame of fire that at one time appeared to glow from within me was all but extinguished.

Oh, it wasn't that I didn't appear spiritual or think of myself as a "good" Christian. Each week I was regularly running two Bible studies and one youth group meeting. I attended church. I was the very active wife of the executive director of Youth for Christ in Cleveland, the mother of a toddler, and the cheerleading coach at a large, local high school. That only proved a point. Not all the things done for God make one godly. So what was missing?

It was just as the first flicker of inner revival was igniting within me that my husband (and boss of seven years) and I left for the weekend to attend the yearly national Youth for Christ convention.

From Flicker to Flame

I always enjoyed a convention. Speakers, singing, challenge. Hmmm. But I needed more than a lift or renewal; I needed fresh power in my life!

Before leaving Cleveland for the convention in Chicago, I had come to the conclusion that this spiritual drought was the result of burnout—overwork, little rest, and too much responsibility. I began to seriously consider leaving ministry. I wanted to be free from outside stress and just be happy inside.

But the first speaker at the convention shocked me with his comment: "If you think it's time to quit, it's too soon!" This had happened to me before. Through a person, God was speaking to me. As if I was the only person in the room, the words from that one sentence resounded and echoed in my ears until I acknowledged that they were directly from God to me.

God seemed to be saying, "Don't get up. Don't go anywhere. Don't daydream or pretend you don't hear My voice. You've been looking for answers, and I'm going to give them to you . . . though perhaps not what you might expect."

Sandwiched between perfect strangers, I didn't dare move. Without a friend to share my experience, I sat back, exhaled, then took the slow, deep breath of a person curious with anticipation. Though somewhat afraid of what God might say or do, I nervously awaited something unusual or supernatural to occur.

Prayer Attitude: Just not a Priority

Then it unfolded as if on cue. Each former president had been asked to share how God had worked in the Youth for Christ (YFC) organization over the previous forty years. Though none of them were given a more specific theme, there was one unexpected thread—especially for my ears—prayer.

Prayer? If the convention had been promoted as a *prayer* conference, I might never have considered attending it. Not that I didn't believe in prayer or its value for the Christian. I just had not, up to that point in time, understood how to make prayer an integral part of my daily walk with Christ. Oh, I "prayed." I kept a journal of written conversations with the Lord, especially on those days when I released an "I need HELP" prayer. And I often found myself asking God for a parking space close to a store entrance during a snowstorm. And I *sometimes* remembered to pray for others' specific needs, but sadly that was the extent of the discipline of prayer in my busy Christian life.

Certainly, young Christians shouldn't be expected to carry on with such a serious (and boring) discipline, should they? Prayer, to be perfectly honest, was not a priority of mine—though it was a spiritual discipline that I believed in and encouraged the students I mentored to practice.

Prayer Action: Make it a Priority!

Like a bombshell, it hit with the second speaker.

Even as he began to share, his sincerity about God, ministry, and prayer became evident. He told of regular, daily intercession for the salvation of his neighbors. I was struck with the thought of his incredibly busy schedule and amazed that he made time to pray for his neighbors. I didn't even know my neighbors' names!

As he continued, his tone of voice rose and his intensity flared as he pounded out the words of James 4:2. Looking at those of us who needed to call on God's power most and probably used it least, he cried, "You do not have because you do not ask! James 4:2." I actually opened my Bible to the verse thinking that it couldn't really say that—at least, not in that way. It wasn't that blatant, was it? Then he choked up with tears and proceeded to impress upon the listeners the fervency of his message: "Prayerlessness, for the believer, is sin."

How he phrased it, said it, or convinced me, I'm still unsure, but the Holy Spirit began His own conviction upon my heart—and never stopped—until the last optional workshop of the convention on Saturday morning. While each godly speaker related their results in prayer—tremendous miracles of healing, incredible circumstances of God's intervention (for example, opening the doors of India to the gospel and YFC after a twenty-four-hour prayer vigil), and even the harvest of souls saved years later *due to daily, consistent prayers*—I cried in silent shame and humiliation through every general session because of my lack of prayer.

Their stories magnified and illuminated my self-sufficient approach to ministry and daily Christian life, as well as convicted me of the sin of prayerlessness. By then, only one word aptly described my state: *ashamed*. I was ashamed of myself for the audacity to lead Bible studies, evangelize, work for God daily, but spend no personal time with Him in conversation or even in confession.

Prayer Application: Not a Choice! Not an Option! A Must!

As the weekend came to a close, we were invited to choose from a list of optional seminars. Like a neon light flashing on the pamphlet was a workshop on prayer. That would be my choice.

As my good friend and I were standing at the entrance to this workshop, laughter seemed appropriate to break up the serious mood of my desire to want to go into a workshop on prayer. Both of us had the feeling that the discipline of prayer was an extremely serious matter, but neither of us leaned toward serious things (at least up to that point in time).

Parting ways, I slowly entered the workshop feeling awkward and hesitant. I picked a seat in the back of the auditorium with the thought that I could leave the room early if it got too serious or boring.

Once again, tears flowed uncontrollably down my cheeks throughout the hour presentation on prayer as the speaker talked of the power available to a believer who prays. To make matters worse, no one else in the room seemed to react to the speaker with similar emotion and my blubbering appeared out of place. I just couldn't pinpoint the root of all of this shame!

But God's work was being completed within me. Through the weekend and culminating with this workshop, I was indeed convinced that prayerlessness in the life of this believer was sin. If I truly believed that spending time with God in prayer was actually engaging in conversation with my Creator, Friend, Savior, Leader, and King, why would I overlook, avoid, forget, or fall asleep in the middle of prayer? If I truly wanted to be used by God to evangelize and disciple the world for Christ, why would I place so little emphasis on time alone with Him?

My perspective on prayer was changing.

I sat frozen as all three hundred workshop attendees filed out of the room. I was definitely the only one in the room with streaked makeup and red puffy cheeks. I just didn't want to leave the room without making dramatic changes in my life. But I didn't know where to start. It seemed overwhelming, beyond my grasp.

Then a woman touched my shoulder, offering to pray with me, about . . .

I bowed my head, determined to make a lifelong decision to . . . to . . . to . . . change, I guess. Change what? Change how?

Then words to God flowed from my mouth with the same intensity and mystery as my initial prayer for salvation had come so desperately from within me seven years earlier. Without pre-meditation, I made a decision in front of God and another person to pray for one hour a day for the rest of my life!

I knew myself too well. If I had given God a trial period to see if "I liked it" or if "it fit into my busy life," I would have allowed the decision to pray an hour a day to fizzle into a sweet memory as a discipline that was "too difficult for me."

No, I sensed God's presence and provision in this decision, and I had been weighing the benefits of prayer in a believer's life versus life without it all week long! It was a hands-down decision to pursue the discipline wholeheartedly.

Searching my mind for something specific, I remembered a number of verses and principles about prayer the speaker had shared. Not a single verse had been new to me—Matthew 6:31-34; 7:7-8; or Philippians 4:6-7, 19. Yet for the first time, those words were alive and fresh and inviting. Their practical-ity pierced me as I realized how they could impact my life on any given day—if I actually believed them! I was stunned by the power they offered.

I told God I would pray for one hour a day for the rest of

my life! I had taken the plunge and I left the room bathed afresh in the power of the Holy Spirit. It was all I could do to find my friend Kinney, go to lunch, and pour out to her all that I felt God was saying to me. Something was coming alive within me. The excitement I had first experienced in my relationship with God as a young Christian had been reignited. That dependency, the willingness to be guided by Him, to listen and to share every thought with Him was bursting from me. In the true style of an evangelist, I elaborated on all that I had heard and all I was certain that God was going to do in my life because of prayer. We laughed, we cried, and both of us remarked how special this convention had been—certain that God had touched our lives.

It was beyond my wildest expectation how God's power would be released into my life from that day forward because of prayer, but first the discipline had to be mastered.

PART II
FROM DECISION
TO DISCIPLINE

CHAPTER
3

KNEE DEEP IN DISCIPLINE

The first morning at home after the convention, without inspirational speakers, great music, or people's faces reminding me of my decision to pray, I walked into my kitchen after sending my son and husband off for the day. A little baffled, I thought: *Well, here I go, my first hour, but where do I start?*

Inexperienced in the classical spiritual disciplines, but not in the gift of gab, I chose to write my prayers. Writing kept me focused, allowing concentration while in conversation with the Lord—much like eye contact intensifies verbal communication—saving me from casual daydreaming and the inevitable distractions of household chores.

Before I sat down, I collected paper and pen and made a fresh pot of coffee. At that very moment, over the radio came the regular jingle of the weekly program, "Chapel of the Air." Speaking was Karen Mains, the same woman who two days earlier and five hundred miles away had led the optional workshop on prayer that was just beginning to rearrange my daily life. To me, it was no coincidence. It was God, in His special and loving way, adding confirmation to my decision. He had heard my convention prayer! Now He was waiting for me.

I turned off the radio, took the phone off the hook, set the alarm on the stove to ring in one hour and had my first "appointment" with God. Afraid I'd run out of things to say before my hour was up, I talked to God about all I could think of (my husband, our ministry, our Campus Life kids, our finances, our friends), then I opened my Bible to read His words and hear His response. He spoke, and as I listened to His gentle, yet firm voice in Scripture, I recorded in writing what He said to me. I sensed that this was a long overdue appointment and I was so grateful to spending time with Him. When the stove alarm buzzed, I was astonished at how quickly the hour had passed and how my spirit was completely refreshed and satisfied.

Immediate Results

That afternoon I proceeded to exercise alone . . . something I had always planned to do on a regular basis but had never been disciplined enough to do. Hmmm. An immediate result to a request in prayer or was it just chance?

No, *chance* was no longer in my vocabulary. Time with God was meant to change my life, to bring

> resolve and
>> results and
>>> revival.

Why wouldn't I experience an immediate change?

I had just asked God to change my desires, even my appetite, to cause me to be disciplined in thought and in body, and I had been encouraged by the Word to pray about everything (Phil. 4:6), to trust God for a "transformed" mind (Rom. 12:2), and to walk blamelessly (Ps. 15) all through the day. Yes, He was speaking to me.

Aah, but that posed a new dilemma. Now the concept of time had much more significance in my daily life. For me to number my days aright (Ps. 90:12) meant that God was interested in my whole day every day—my errands and appointments, what I watched on TV or listened to on the radio, even how long I spent chatting on the phone.

I began to take a good look at my habits, choices, opportunities, interruptions, and commitments with a new, much more discerning mind. It seemed that every hour of every day mattered to God. And David in Psalm 139 seemed to validate this principle by stating that God had preplanned our days even before our birth. Certainly, then, I should consult Him on how to spend my day.

Soap operas and other daytime television shows were immediately out of the schedule—a waste of precious time. Even my husband thought they were ridiculous, though he had never asked me not to watch them. But as if the timing was right for my stubborn little spirit to be willing, he suggested that I no longer watch soap operas. I agreed, thinking there was much more I could do with my time, so I made a decision with him that I would never watch them again.

But one day I seemed terribly bored, and I sheepishly turned the television on . . . just to see what was happening on "General Hospital." As my toddler and I were sitting on the floor in front of the TV, I heard a car pull into the driveway. My husband, who rarely came home during the day, proceeded to walk through the front door. I jumped up to change the channel, abruptly decided to turn the TV off, ran to the radio, and pretended as if I had not been watching TV. Immediately, I sensed that I was going to begin a very deceitful practice if I continued this process. That little scenario was enough to convince me to never watch soap operas again.

Within days, daydreaming about losing weight and inches was replaced with exercise. I even began to look forward to releasing my anxieties and tensions through fun workouts, rather than dreading the discipline. I was suddenly ready and willing to change the physical area of my life, but prior to my commitment to pray an hour a day, I was unable to make myself do what I needed and wanted to do to improve my health.

Looking for a local aerobics class, rekindled a relationship with my best friend from elementary school and we enjoyed spiritual growth as well as companionship and accountability in our exercise schedule. She would pick me up for aerobics class three times a week, or we'd exercise to a video at one of our homes. We counted on each other to stay disciplined, yet maintained a personal inner drive to achieve our fitness goals. Discipline was infiltrating every area of my life.

Christian talk radio filled many hours of my day instead of secular music or daytime television talk shows. Now, life with God was not just my occupation, but my preoccupation as well. My inner fire was burning brightly!

Before long, it was apparent that prayer must occur in the earliest part of my day, otherwise distractions, such as phone calls, laundry, even family members needing something to eat, interrupted that quiet hour with God. Among other things, I had to give up my habit of "sleeping in." Prayer became an appointment on my calendar; and it had to be both planned for and kept. Had this appointment been with anyone else—friend, student, or businessperson—I would have had the same professional concerns and made the same courteous efforts of being on time, prepared, alert, and attentive. Therefore, I daily kept an "appointment" frame of mind in planning my hour with God. And on those inevitable days when things just didn't go as I planned, the decision to pray an hour a day, made in that seminar room months earlier, kept me accountable. I either stayed up late or hid away during midday. I was determined!

More Immediate Results

One hour a day in prayer produced undeniable answers to specific requests! Most especially, prayer began to produce a personal transformation with such positive differences in my character and lifestyle that even my family noticed. Not only did I crack the dawn, waking often before my alarm and tip-toeing out of the bedroom rather than following my usual "hit the snooze three times for extra sleep" habit, but I began to hold my temper in check with my toddler instead of becoming unreasonably angry.

Equally surprising, but perhaps not as pleasant, prayer uncovered personality flaws that had been swept under the rug, shoved aside, and denied for many years, revealing an escape artist's tactics in avoiding God's correction or conviction. But with daily prayer, what once seemed too painful or personal to admit (such as a competitive jealousy toward others, uncontrolled anger, and even the firm grasp unforgiveness had upon my emotions), now was approachable. When I willingly exposed these flaws to my loving Father and over time disposed of them with His help, my friendships blossomed, unhealthy inclinations to compete and compare were either reproved or diminished, and my self-image vastly improved.

Prayer was no longer a drudgery that I considered boring or for the elderly; it was becoming an attainable, alluring, healing, spiritual discipline I was excited to pursue. Now I was cookin'!

Teach Me to Pray with Power!

I had only scratched the surface of understanding more about the dynamics of prayer when an insatiable appetite for reading books on the subject consumed me. I began rummaging through shelves at my office and in our home, looking for books on prayer.

I found books on prayer I never realized I had and I was certain I hadn't purchased! I couldn't tell you where I got them. This mystery became one more sign of God's hand teaching me, leading me to pray.

I discovered a thirty-year-old, yellow-paged classic by a long-gone, but greatly respected pastor, Andrew Murray, who wrote much about prayer. One morning the title of his book, *The Prayer Life*, caught my eye. I slipped it from its row on a shelf beside my bed, where it must have been shelved unnoticed for years, and leafed through the first, fifth, twentieth, then forty-fifth page. Before I realized it, I was sitting on the floor reading for over half an hour. Engrossed, I could hardly believe what I was uncovering.

Detailed in this very old book was the account of how Andrew Murray's life was renewed and ignited afresh when he discovered the power unleashed through prayer. From that point, he began to write much about the discipline of prayer as an incredibly dynamic source of power for the believer, especially the minister, but one that is most neglected. I gasped as I recognized I had just walked through this very journey! Even in the foreword I could see the similarity between my experience and Andrew Murray's experience of having been in ministry and feeling powerless. He, along with other ministers in 1912 in South Africa, identified prayerlessness as the deep-rooted problem resulting in a lack of spiritual power in their denomination.

He wrote, "Prayer is in every deed the pulse of spiritual life. It is the great means of bringing to minister and people the blessing and power of heaven. Persevering and believing prayer means a strong and abundant life."

He went on to say that once the "spirit of confession began

to prevail," meaning that once each individual confessed and repented of prayerlessness, they began to expect victory over all that, in the past, had hindered their prayer lives.

I, too, was finding a fiery newness in my relationship with Jesus Christ that no longer allowed me to ignore my constant need for His influence, power, teaching, or thoughts in my life that came through prayer. Wow! How long had I lived without this power available to my life? Too long!

This little book described the journey of prayerlessness, the fight to overcome it, and the blessings available when we gain victory over it. Andrew Murray gave biblical examples of Jesus' prayer life and explained how the Holy Spirit was a prompter to prayer and that the results of prayer in a believer's life would be obedience and even powerful preaching. The benefits would be overflowing. It was incredible, exciting, and stirring.

But Andrew Murray wasn't the only one who had once neglected prayer. Peter Marshall, former chaplain of the Senate in the 1940's, also confessed that neglect of prayer was his personal loss. He declared, "The whole field of prayer, and praying as laying hold on unlimited power, is unexplored, with the result that spiritual laws still lie undiscovered by the average believer." And he added that "sometimes, in our desperation, we hit upon the right way to pray, and things happen—our prayers are gloriously answered. But for the most part, our praying is very haphazard, and the results are often disappointing."

It wasn't long before I was soaking up antiquated books on prayer. They motivated me to uncover as much as I could about this lost art! I uncovered incredible hidden treasures in other author's lives such as O. Hallesby who said, "Neglect prayer. Neglect God." Each book, each quote, each author increased my firm determination to cling to a daily appointment with God.

It was as if I had been blind and now my eyes were suddenly opened. I was convinced that prayer was an essential lifelong discipline for a Christian to embrace. Once again and with childlike delight, I was making Jesus my constant companion. He was the One I could talk to, cry with, complain to, or seek advice from. I learned *not* to wish or worry, but to simply pray!

During my daily hour of quiet time with the Lord, writing my conversations to Him, listening for His response by reading the Word, a new, inner strength developed. I encountered God daily, discovering something fresh about His character and receiving a boldness to believe Him for more and more power in my life. I found an unrestrained enthusiasm from sharing my faith with strangers—whether I was standing at the checkout counter in the grocery store, talking to the postman, coaching at the local high school, or in any situation. Each moment of my life seemed to have a purpose. I would ask myself, *"What would Jesus have me do right now? What would He have me say?"* I didn't feel timid or directionless or weak.

But inevitably, by the end of each day, I sensed my spirit needed renewal, exhortation, and direction. And as weak as I would come to my daily appointment with God, I would leave twice as strong and with a deep desire to pull others toward Him.

During my hour with God, I would receive the detailed directions for my day—His plan and the promise of His Holy Spirit's power to guide me. "Marching orders," as Peter Marshall called God's specific will for one's daily life, created great excitement in me that was evidenced by many! Phone calls long awaited would ring in, ministry and business decisions snapped into place, and I would constantly whisper to myself, "He did it. Just as He said, just as He promised." And the more answers to prayer, change of circumstances, healings, and mended relationships that would occur, the more vocal I became about my daily appointment with God.

"I've Gotta Tell Everyone"

At first people would just humor me, thinking my child-like faith was "cute." But with each passing day and "you won't believe what God did" story, their expressions and questions grew more serious.

"You don't really pray for one hour, do you?"

"That was just a coincidence, don't you think?"

"Maybe you shouldn't tell so many people you pray an hour a day. That sounds too pious."

But soon, it was, "Umm, Becky, would you pray for me? My . . ."

Even my relationship with my husband and God became more intimate. Roger had taught me to write my prayers as a young Christian, and he daily practiced what he preached through all the years of our marriage by journaling his prayers. Therefore, when I made such a radical time commitment to pray, he watched with interest as each day passed. Because I was so sensitive now to God's voice, I would say, "God spoke to me," and he cautioned me, suggesting that I say, "I feel as if God is showing me . . ." His wise advice allowed me the freedom to practice listening to God and sometimes fail, and it also allowed me to be corrected and accountable to others whom God had put in my life as mentors, adding credibility to my accounts of conversations with God.

In listening to God's voice as a couple, we felt that His individual counsel to us would be similar. If there was ever a discrepancy, we would continue seeking God until Roger and I both felt Him saying the *same thing* to us (in relationship to ministry, family, or our future). We would continue to look for scriptural confirmation or additional circumstances, waiting for the Holy Spirit to sway one of us—to make a unanimous decision of three!

One such time was shortly after the birth of our son, Jacob. Roger felt God wanted us to have another child. I had barely recovered from the first tough delivery, and I panicked. At that point, he and I differed dramatically on what we felt God was saying to us.

Since we had reached an impasse, I suggested we make an appointment with our pastor. That seemed a risky thing to do because our pastor had nine children! But after meeting and praying with us, our pastor suggested that, because of my high level of anxiety, immediately having another child would not be in the best for our relationship. Relieved and feeling God's direction and comfort through our pastor, we put the issue on hold and regularly brought it up for reconsideration. (For the record, we never had another child!)

Within a few short months, prayer was noticeably changing every facet of my life *and* releasing the power of God that was both undeniable and appealing. Reading and rereading Andrew Murray's many books on prayer unveiled the words, "Prayer is the secret of power and life. Not only for ourselves, but for others, for the church, for the world; it is to prayer that God has given the right to take hold of Him and His strength. It is on prayer that the promises wait for their fulfillment." Not only was I *learning to pray*, but every area of my life was changing because of prayer!

CHAPTER

4

CHANGE YOUR PRIORITIES, POSSIBILITIES, PERSONALITY, AND PERSPECTIVES THROUGH PRAYER

Priorities

Perhaps the most obvious impact of a daily appointment with the Lord was the fact that one more hour found its way into an already packed schedule. The once-hectic lifestyle of carpool mom, youth worker, cheerleading coach, and wife found an anchor by beginning each day with an hour of written prayer. This "Type-A," overly committed woman was forced to change her priorities if she was going to walk her talk.

It became a conscious commitment to pencil onto my calendar *one day in advance* what "hour" I was going to pray on the following day. In planning out my day (workouts, lunch appointments, business and ministry meetings, or other commitments), I was no longer looking for time with God; I was *making* time for God. How true the statement became, "If you don't have time for God, you don't have time!" But it was more; I was learning to give God time. As Andrew Murray said, "God needs time with us. If we would only give Him time . . . to exercise the full influence of His presence on us."

His presence through the Word and times in prayer "worked on me" to change a negative attitude when I was stubborn or to release an unmet expectation or disappointment. He motivated me when I was procrastinating to complete a promise or confront a difficult situation. He *guided* me with ideas, creativity, and specific direction for completing short and long term projects.

My appointments with God were definitely
    changing my priorities,
        pushing away the clutter, and
            revealing the difference between
                the urgent and the important.

I changed from being someone who failed to plan and did not see *any* results to becoming someone who was an organized planner of my time, ultimately accomplishing my goals. Planning, goal setting, and time management suddenly became subjects of great interest to me. Why? Because time in conversation with God produced ideas that seemed reachable and exciting. They had God-confidence behind them. Each morning I had to choose whether I would consider those thoughts as something that "could be," or would I take those ideas as implanted within me by God and act upon them?

Initially I would hear God speak to me about practically helping others. I had a Christian friend who was getting psychiatric counseling. I didn't know how I could help, and I would avoid the thought that God wanted me to do something until it grew loud and clear. As if I could not ignore God's prodding any longer, I felt I needed to extend a visual expression of my love and concern for my friend. The idea to send flowers to her came one morning during my quiet time. I did not usually send flowers to others, nor was there such an item in our limited budget. Yet, I asked my husband what he thought of sending a cheery bouquet of flowers to our mutual, hurting friend. His immediate agreement signaled to both of us that, though out of the ordinary, this idea seemed God-inspired and we should gladly proceed. When our friend called that afternoon after receiving the bouquet, we could almost see the smile on her face and hear the joy that had been missing in her voice for weeks!

That was just the start of what "giving" ideas would come out of time in prayer. Though we had tithed since our wedding day, I always seemed to give—no more, no less than 10 percent—with reservation and without a willing spirit.

One Christmas, my prayers focused on giving *cheerfully*. Why couldn't I? Why didn't I? Why did I find the act of giving so difficult? I had assumed that the spiritual gift of giving was not a gift I possessed; therefore, I was inclined to give out of duty. But that way of thinking was being challenged by the Word of God as it washed through my daily thoughts and caused me to examine my motives.

I purposed to change that area of my life. Then, as always, when I became willing to change, an opportunity arose for me to act.

We put our house up for sale only a few months after I determined to become a more cheerful giver. It was at the same time that a Jamaican missionary wanted desperately to attend the Billy Graham Evangelists Conference in Europe. He did not have any money and did not know anyone who could financially help him, except for me, because I had been his small group leader in his Youth for Christ program years earlier.

When my missionary friend boldly asked me for five hundred dollars (which I did not have), it appeared more than likely that God prodded him to call upon me, providing me with an opportunity to stretch my faith, give willingly, and obey Him. In addition, he needed the money by a certain date. In faith I believed that we would certainly sell our house by the time he needed the money. Without thinking of the consequences or even consulting my husband about how much we would sell our house for or how much profit would be made, I told my Jamaican friend that I would send him 10 percent of the earnings from the sale of our house in time for him to attend the Billy Graham Conference.

After I hung up the phone, I asked my husband if that was okay. He looked at me with one of those looks that only a husband can give after a wife has put her foot in her mouth and said, "I guess it's going to have to be okay." At that point I got down on my knees and asked God if He would quickly sell our house. I told Him we would give 10 percent of our earnings to our friend who needed it by that summer. When all was said and done, it was exactly 10 percent of our profit that was sent "just in time" for our Jamaican friend to attend the conference in Europe! That experience was a turning point in trusting God to arrange the priorities of my life. I was certainly stretched to believe that I could be a cheerful giver and that God would help me in the process.

Time in prayer led to action steps that needed to be carried out in a disciplined fashion unto completion. Calendars, to-do lists, phone calls, and correspondence—all needed to be included in a day's work where previously watching television, telephoning, and pursuing other time wasters had achieved little for the kingdom of God.

Becky, Know Your "Call"!

As my renewed priorities fell into place, my life's purpose gained shape. I began to take daily steps toward those things I hoped for but could not see, looking forward to their completion with expectation. The priorities once placed on luncheons, recreation, meetings, and even sleep all needed reevaluating and adjusting *because* of prayer. At one time, I would say "yes" to almost every request. Now when an opportunity arose, an interruption occurred, or a door opened, I weighed its importance on the basis of my personal call in life as a wife, mom, youth worker, author, or speaker, *prayerfully* considering its priority before making a decision. The more often I'd make wrong choices, the more quickly I learned to make the right choices regarding the use of my time. Overbooking my calendar with too much activity, saying yes too often to the "good, but not the best," not meeting deadlines, and being late for appointments because I miscalculated driving times or answering the phone when I shouldn't have done so, were painful and sometimes humiliating lessons. But their sting caused me to increase my awareness of God's plan for my daily life in relationship to my life's purpose and often pushed me into another timely transition. The outcome? Firm decisions came more easily and responses to requests came more rapidly. My ability to discern God's will for my life grew sharper.

Little did I know just how much my life would change when I made a simple decision to pray for an hour each day!

After recognizing the disorganized lifestyle I had been maintaining and groping my way back to a healthier, more disciplined condition, I discovered excellent tools for speedy recovery and growth. Guiding me to evaluate and manage my time were experts such as Anne Ortlund's *Disciplines of a Beautiful Woman*, Ted Engstrom with *The Pursuit of Excellence*, and Gordon Mac-Donald's *Ordering Your Private World*. In Mac-Donald's "memo to the disorganized" it almost seemed as simple as this: "If my private world is in order, it will be because I'm convinced that the inner world of the spiritual must govern the outer world of activity." I came to believe that time is important to God and godly use of time should be important to the believer. What will our daily lives look like if we don't consult the Spirit of God to give us wisdom, affirmation, encouragement, direction, and guidance in place of the world's noise, confusion, and disorganization?

In *Ordering Your Private World* I discovered a description of a life lived out of prayer: "Finally at the center we are filled by the power and strength of God as Holy Spirit. There is a resurgence of confidence and expectancy. We receive insight and wisdom; faith that removes mountains is generated, and our love for others, even for the unlovable, begins to grow." Isn't that what it is all about? These books thoroughly convinced me that every hour of a Christian's life is valuable to God, and they equally convinced me that wasting time was certainly an expensive and inexcusable loss of time!

Possibilities

As my priorities realigned themselves, my vision cleared and I could see forever! Time with God proved invaluable in the area of dreaming big dreams and believing that with God's help they were possible, even though (especially as a former alcoholic) a shadow of the past tended to overshadow any self-confidence and adventuresome spirit within me that dared to dream. Nevertheless, having lacked the necessary discipline for turning dreams into reality *prior* to my hour meetings with God, I was astonished at a newfound sense of determination and endurance to achieve what once seemed improbable or impossible.

Over and over again, I would have the idea to speak at an event, meet a person, visit a special place, or even turn my spoken testimony into an article—even a book! And for as many times as I would shove the idea aside, it would return. I then heard a pastor share, "If an idea doesn't go away, begin to treat it as if it is from God. Let *Him* bring it to pass." My appointments with God often
> contained conversations
>> that turned into hopes,
>>> then became goals that structured plans
>>>> and ultimately turned into accomplishments.

I even surprised myself with the action steps I would take to see a dream fulfilled, especially when the odds were stacked against me. Once, in a conversation with a book distributor, I was told "no" to an idea simply because there was no previous sales record for that type of product.

Yet, if the distributor would accept my product, I had an offer from a large company to sell my product—beginning with a (large for me) minimum order of 350 units. Seeing this immediate opportunity falling apart in front of me, I basically said to the fellow on the other end of the line whom I'd never met, "You can't say, 'No.'" He said, "Lady, you don't have a track record." I said, "What's a track record?" He remarked, "Proven sales." I said, "But I just sold 500 units in a local store in just two months! Isn't that enough?" He said, "Well, not for a national distributor." I said, "If you say 'no' to me, I will not have an opportunity to fill this order. You just can't say 'no.' You have to give me a chance." Then slowly and with reservation he asked, "Lady, how much is each unit?" We made an initial agreement that he would order 350, and within two months he had ordered an additional 1,000 units.

From the thought to call a person or to suggest a direction in a meeting or to send a manuscript to a publisher, my possibilities became realities, and my faith was constantly stretched to step out into new areas of trusting God.

Scriptures on faith increased the assuredness that this recent result of time with God (dreaming!) was not unusual activity, but one that had been lying dormant just waiting to be released. Instead of being timid or insecure that these ideas—some *looking* impossible—were not from God, I adopted more of the "Philippians 4" attitude: "I can do all things through Christ who strengthens me." And though initially I may have looked foolish or even arrogant to dream big dreams, I sensed God's assuredness filling me.

As days and weeks and even months would pass without an outward sign I was indeed moving in *God's* direction, I would cling to the Word and my faith, fueled by the Holy Spirit's conviction that what I believed God had planned for my life would indeed come to pass. I sometimes felt ridiculous—like Noah must have felt with onlookers smirking at his eccentric faith. At other times I felt indignant—like Jonah thinking, *"Why do I have to do this?"* And I often felt abandoned—like Joseph must have felt in prison—because of others' reactions to the "dreams" he believed God had given him.

Yet always God's answers came through in His time, whisking me even more confidently into another adventure with Him. Because He had proven His faithfulness through innumerable circumstances, dreaming God's possibilities became my regular practice. A one-time daydreamer, I was now a dreamer determined to follow through each day with God's plan for my life—no matter how impossible! This was such an exciting, unexpected, and powerful result of my daily appointment with God.

Personality

Weak, insecure, easily angered, jealous, selfish, and *lazy* were all words that described my personality prior to hourly appointments with God. Not that those negative qualities vanished forever, but the more I prayed, the more I possessed a new and strong censorship of those characteristics by the Holy Spirit within me. It was not only temper outbursts, cold looks, or an outer hardness that faded, but what once seemed semi-acceptable behavior for a Christian (cutting remarks, mild gossip, or loose slang) now elicited a holy poke from within me. Through the years following my conversion, I reverted to many "old nature" habits or manipulation, moodiness, harbored resentments, bitterness, and jealousies. Not long after I had allowed the discipline of prayer to impact my outward life, I was confronted (almost bombarded) with my sickly inner life—one needing healing and health! Many hours of prayer revealed much sin, and lots of tears. Endless conversations with God brought much confession and ultimately, restoration.

Since my conversion experience in 1976, I had been fully aware of the Holy Spirit's power, gifts, and manifestations, but I had not consciously invited the person of the Holy Spirit into my daily walk for years. Now my renewed belief in Him as a powerful person within me, rather than a ghostly entity floating about haphazardly, prompted me to regularly call upon the Holy Spirit and submit to His available strength and power.

As if I had lost touch with a close friend, I felt remorse at my stupidity and ignorance of leaving Him out of my life. I became quicker to sense sin in my thought life—doubts, malice, envy, or jealousy—and the Spirit and my "flesh" often went to war.

No longer could I casually speed without noticing the speedometer; I'd feel the blush of red cheeks that accompanies doing something wrong, and then I'd tap on the brakes. I could no longer relate something to a friend and conveniently omit a fact that would embarrass me because an immediate guilty verdict would pound in my ears. For instance, if I had forgotten to give someone a message that I was responsible for relaying, I could no longer say, "Oh, I couldn't get hold of that person," or make up an excuse because the Holy Spirit would bring the truth quickly to my mind so that I had to speak it. I could no longer spank my son out of anger without sensing that I was just as wrong in the situation by being an out-of-control parent. I was even caught by a principal who said to me, "Well, how many missed the practice?" when I had exaggerated by saying, "Everyone missed the practice." I realized that I needed to speak the truth at all times.

Not only my mouth, but my "eyes" were under scrutiny. I

would feel a dull pain in my stomach when I watched a movie or television show that would elicit strong memories of my old life . . . the sensual, fast-paced, lifestyle of young Americans today. I could no longer watch certain TV programs or movies without dwelling on the lustful aspects of them. They only produced a negative influence over my thought life and immediate contradictions within me.

Slowly, the Holy Spirit began to gain the upper hand and control the "flesh" within me as long as I would moment-by-moment acknowledge, call upon, and invite His indwelling power to fill me.

Though the "indwelling" was obviously supernatural and invisible, I chose to believe the Holy Spirit was transforming my personality, and I consciously asked Him to do so daily in prayer.

The result? As often as both hidden and obvious unholy habits and ugly personality flaws surfaced in my life, I asked God to change and heal me. And as often as I would come under the control of the Holy Spirit, those habits and flaws were eventually flushed out. I was daily being refined, conformed, cleansed, and forgiven through prayer. A newer, softer person was emerging after each appointment with God.

Perspectives

Not only did prayer and its phenomenal results cause my perspective of prayer to drastically change, but my perspective of God truly changed as well.

Not that I hadn't felt God's love toward me, but an emotional love *toward Him* was developing as a result of my time in prayer. How could it be any different? Spending so much time with anyone develops a solid friendship and trust. God never ceased to amaze me nor did He ever disappoint me. Oh, I was disappointed in *my* unmet expectations when I would infringe upon His character by *telling* Him how or when to answer a prayer rather than *asking* Him to meet my needs, but nothing He ever promised did He withdraw from me or fail to perform. His unfailing love and faithful, loyal character became my strength. I wanted to be around Him as often as possible, and He continually proved His trustworthiness through daily intervention. He was gentle and comforting when I fell apart, needed help, or had to start over. I wanted to know His will and was not afraid to ask Him to show me.

Each transition in my life seemed heralded by a trumpeter when a circumstance would occur to change the course of my life or when I would meet a new friend or bump into a perfect stranger who would become the missing piece in the puzzle of my life.

Once, while I was sitting in a youth workers training retreat, a guest speaker nonchalantly mentioned an organization she was affiliated with—C.L.A.S.S. (Christian Leaders and Speakers Seminars). The mere mention of the name C.L.A.S.S. (unrelated to her purpose in being there) triggered something within me to find out more. I had *daily* been asking God to give me the skills to speak the message of my testimony, so I requested a brief appointment with the speaker, and upon returning home from the retreat, I immediately followed up on the whereabouts of the next and nearest C.L.A.S.S.

That "coincidence" resulted in training, traveling, and a teacher-mentor relationship with Florence and Fred Littauer, founders of C.L.A.S.S. and authors of numerous Christian books.

Another time, I had *daily* been asking the Lord to open doors for me to speak to students. Having relocated, I was so new to the West Coast of the United States that I hardly knew where to begin to build contacts. Attending a National Youth Workers Convention in San Francisco seemed a good beginning, but anonymity in a large convention hall was overwhelming. In the very last hour of the convention I clumsily bumped into the cofounder of Youth Specialties, Mike Yaconelli, and that initial, spontaneous conversation resulted in almost a decade of speaking opportunities to students and youth workers.

I realized only One person knew me so well and still loved me so much! I became vividly aware that God was my ever-present Counselor, Friend and Father.

I learned that prayer is not a monologue to a deaf God, but a conversation with a God who hears prayer.

Prayer is not helping God with an answer; it is asking God to help. It is not telling God what to do; it is telling Him my needs. It isn't so much for the disciplined as for the undisciplined!

Prayer is not necessarily meant to be an easy joy ride, but it definitely is a spiritual discipline that produces joy!

Prayer is not just coming to Jesus; it is letting Jesus come into me!

Prayer is not only for the educated, seminary scholar; it is for anyone who will practice, persevere, and plan to pray!

Prayer is not a substitute for time in the Word; it will lead to the Word.

Prayer is not for the impatient, but for the one who waits!

Prayer is not a place to boast, but a place to confess.

Prayer is not my motivating God, but God motivating me.

Prayer is not a waste of time; it is an appointment with the King of kings!

My perspective of prayer and God changed!

The initial discovery months earlier—that power is released when one prays and that prayerlessness is sin—prompted me to make a non-negotiable, no-turning-back decision to pray for one hour a day. After the decision had become a daily discipline, affecting every area of my life, I desperately needed to get that hour of prayer organized so that I could be, as James 5:16 stated, a powerful and effective pray-er!

CHAPTER 5

HOW TO PRAY
THE "WRITE" WAY

It wasn't long before I understood that to be a successful pray-er I needed to . . .

prepare my heart for prayer,
plan my time in prayer, and
practice the art of prayer.

Prepare Your Heart

Have an attitude of anticipation.

Before each prayer appointment, it is extremely helpful to picture yourself actually sitting across the table from Jesus. Imagine Him grasping your hand or touching your shoulder, wiping a tear, smiling warmly, laughing softly, or raising His eyebrows during your conversation. These thoughts will increase your affection and intimacy with God!

He wants to meet with you!

Perhaps you have the misconception that God is far away from you in heaven; or that He is not personal, but an entity, unfamiliar and distant. Maybe you feel awkward initiating transcendental thoughts that bounce out to nowhere or stay within the four walls of a room that reach no one.

To prepare your heart for prayer is to *expect* His presence in your meeting, to wait in anticipation for Him and His responses. King David modeled "written" prayer with his passionate recorded appeals to the One he knew and loved through much of the book of Psalms, his prayer journal. He was very personal and intimate with his God. Through the Psalms, we are given a pattern to follow; we learn how to come to God with an attitude of expectancy, believing that He will meet us, hear us, and answer us!

Not to expect anything from God just might be exactly what you get, and it won't be long before "time with God" becomes a tedious duty. But if each day, you anticipate new revelations from Him and are bold to pour your heart out to Him, He will not—cannot—disappoint you.

Why "Abide in Him" Daily?

In John 15, Jesus discusses the vine and branches with His disciples. In different New Testament versions, the key phrase is either "abide" or "remain in Me." If you replace either of those phrases with "spend time with Me," you have the following reasons for having a regular, daily appointment with God:

1. If you spend time with God, He will spend time with you (v. 4).
2. You *cannot* bear fruit unless you spend time with God (v. 4).
3. But you will bear much fruit if you spend time with Him (v. 5).
4. Anyone who does not spend time with God will be thrown away like a branch, picked up, thrown into the fire, and burned (v. 6).
5. If you spend time with Him and His words spend time

in you, "Ask whatever you wish, and it will be given you" (v. 7).

6. Now spend time enjoying God's love (v. 9)!

    It appears clear that Jesus wants us:

    • To spend time with Him to further His kingdom.
    • To receive His love.
    • To be empowered to do His works.
    • To know Him and His ways so intimately that whatever we ask will be given to us!

Jesus encourages us to spend time with Him daily in order to know Him better and more fully know His will for our lives. And He clearly invites us to ask of Him in prayer.

Plan Your Start: Have a Plan to Abide

If you clearly understand *Whom* you are meeting and *why*, then *where*, *when*, and *how* are the next questions to answer in order to have a powerful daily appointment with God.

Where?

Have a few favorite places to meet with God daily—out in the yard, at the breakfast table, at your office desk, in a library, overlooking a valley or lake, by a garden window, or even by the fireplace. Set the atmosphere with either complete silence or soft, instrumental music. The habit of meeting with God in the same place develops a consistent pattern.

For best results, assess where you will be least interrupted and most comfortable for a specific period of time. Make that your appointed place to spend time with God.

When?

I found that morning hours afford quiet, uninterrupted time with God—before the phone rings and chores or responsibilities are required. Earlier on some days than others, my appointment with God increased my awareness of His plan for each day, giving Him ample opportunity to influence my upcoming decisions and choices, as well as allowing me the renewal and fresh start that confession and forgiveness offer. My research showed that the "morning watch," as Andrew Murray called his preferred time with God, was the earliest hour of the day, before a day's work had begun. It was also the time of day most often suggested for prayer by those "giants of God" recorded in the Bible and in historical spiritual biographies.

How?

I personally recommend, for a variety of reasons, that you set aside a *specific* amount of time as a minimum standard for your daily appointment with God. First, the accountability to a set amount of time allows you to plan realistically for your appointment with God. Second, it increases your probability of keeping the appointment. And finally, the structure of a time block prompts you to set an alarm earlier, go to bed earlier, or excuse yourself if necessary in order to protect your time with God.

My personal experience proved that when life got inevitably and unusually busy or I was out of town or on vacation, having "no set time" with God, dwindled down to "no time at all" with God. And if I ever had extra time, it was always a pleasure to enjoy leisurely appointments with God. Though I was not naturally a "plan ahead" person, I gained confidence and comfort by setting a specific amount of time aside for my appointment with God. In fact, for me, anything less than one hour was not long enough to incorporate all aspects of my two-way conversations with God (admission, requests, listening to Him through Bible reading, etc.)

Adhering to a specific amount of time to daily talk and listen to God simply made me consistent in keeping my commitment to be with Him! (If you, like me, become convinced that you need more of God in every area of your life, you will have to overcome laziness and procrastination by making a non-negotiable decision of your will to spend significant time with Him.)

Practice Your Part

Practice, practice, practice.

Written prayer was a black and white transcript of my conversations with God. I could look back and review a day or a week or a year in my journey with God. I learned to pray specifically; with perseverance, hope, and faith. I could retrace times when I thought God was not answering a prayer only to see it as a delay and not a denial. I could review the journey of a prayer request—its evolution from where it started, how my desires changed (or *were* changed by God), and how its final answer was always timely, exciting, and often exhilarating.

Practicing prayer, like any sport or discipline, took
- Time and effort
- A scheduled appointment on my calendar
- Regular review and evaluation
- Variety added into my training program
- Additional training on a regular basis
- Built-in accountability factors
- Goals
- A reward program

Prayer became such an integral part of my daily life that I didn't realize that I was progressing through stages of beginner, intermediate, and advanced; improving with time and practice. The more I prayed, the more confident I became as a pray-er, moving from . . .

>fear to faith,
>>doubt to trust, and
>>>intimidation to boldness.

For me, "written" prayer kept my appointments with God alive, personal, conversational, spontaneous, emotional, and adventuresome!

PART III

THE DESIGN
FOR PRAYER

CHAPTER

6

ONE CHRISTIAN'S SECRET TO A HAPPY HOUR

Three months after I had made the decision to pray for one hour a day and had mastered the discipline by writing my prayers and recording God's responses, I knew I needed a sense of order.

One Monday morning, I stared out my kitchen window while seated at my regular quiet time spot with pen, paper, highlighter, and Bible. It was still dark outside, and I almost hoped for Jesus to walk up the sidewalk and join me for coffee and toast. Some days I would ache for the touch of His hand or the sound of His voice to guide me. I whispered, "Couldn't You just come here and show me or tell me exactly how to pray?"

I needed a plan. I needed both accountability and organization. As if spoken by God in response to my comment (or was it a complaint?), James 4:2 came to my mind: "You do not have, because you do not ask God." So I asked God for an idea.

I should have known then to take God at His word, for the next conversation that took place between us resulted in dreaming, designing, ordering, speaking, forming a small business, and selling over fourteen thousand notebooks within the following few years (and eventually over 250,000 *My Partner*

Prayer Notebooks over the next two decades).

God had given me an idea. It came like gushing water released from a pipe that had broken loose. My pen wrote as fast as the thoughts and ideas came, leaving little room for inquiries of my own to interrupt God's thoughts to me:

> Develop a notebook, a three-ring binder, call it *My Partner*, use it each morning, carry it everywhere, and consider it a companion to your Bible. It will have two Parts:

MY PART of the notebook would have four sections, P.A.R.T., to journal my prayers. The first section, PRAISE, was for devotional reading, studying, and rewriting four to five psalms a day, making them my personal praise prayers. The Psalms taught me to open up my time with God in His Word.

In the next section, ADMIT, I honestly discussed my temper, impatience, and other problems and concerns with the One who already knew them. I found Him always waiting for me to confess and be cleansed from any known sin. (Not a day went by when I didn't have a journal entry in this section!) By confessing my sins in writing every day, I gained assurance that integrity, blamelessness, and holiness were assets in the life of a believer, not burdens to run from, but characteristics toward which I should strive. I daily wrote the words of Psalm 139:23-24 and always left the ADMIT section of *My Partner Prayer Notebook* encouraged and prompted by the promise of Romans 12:2—asking and expecting God's Holy Spirit to daily renew my mind.

Psalm 5:3 described the third section, REQUESTS:

> In the morning, O LORD, you hear my voice; in

the morning I lay my requests before you and wait
in expectation.

Each morning I laid my requests before God and waited
expectantly for His reply, aware that "a request may or may not
be granted"—as reminded by C. S. Lewis. The expectation that
my prayer requests would be considered by God became great
training ground for my faith to mature.

Finally, in the THANKS section, I daily acknowledged to
God in writing that I recognized His touch, love, and intimacy
in my life through all the circumstances, interventions, and answers to specific requests arranged by His hand; they were not
by chance!

GOD'S PART to me came in the form of an acrostic—
L.M.N.O.P. "L" was the section of my notebook specifically
set aside for planned times of contemplative LISTENING to
God. "M" was the MESSAGES section, where I kept notes of
powerful teaching times in class settings, during sermons, or
even while reading great books. And "N.O.P." were sections
I used for recording verses from the NEW and OLD TESTA-
MENTS and the book of PROVERBS that either comforted or
convicted me. The last tab in the notebook, making ten sections, was labeled "TO DO." Often, during my morning appointment with God, I would be reminded of people to call,
visit, or write, so I used this section to record, rather than rush
off to do (or even forget), those ideas.

My system for talking and listening to God through the
sections of *My Partner Prayer Notebook* took one hour. Could
it be a coincidence? Surely not in my mind!

My hour with God became a very thorough, conversational
counseling appointment. I was daily growing to understand
the spiritual discipline of prayer, its incredible importance in
the life of a believer, more of God's character, the concept of

faith, and the practicality of time spent in written conversation with God.

Only time would reveal how a little prayer notebook could change my life!

REQUESTS

Ask and it will be given to you; seek and you will find; knock and the door will be opened to you. For everyone who asks receives; he who seeks finds; and to him who knocks, the door will be opened. Matthew 7:7, 8

There are a number of Scripture verses similar to Matthew 7:7,8 that encourage you to ask God for His plan and will for your life. Philippians 4:6 invites us to pray about everything, rather than to worry! And Matthew 6:31-34 describes how many of us worry about things like clothes, food and drink, but in verse 33, Jesus says, "But seek first his kingdom and his righteousness, and all these things will be given to you as well."

What does it mean to "seek God first"? It means to look, search for and pursue Him and His plans for your life. And what better way to search for His will than through a daily prayer two-way conversation with Him?

God wants us to ask Him for His will. In James 4:2, we read, "You do not have, because you do not ask God." Do you believe this? The goal of this section is to provide a written record of your requests made to God, as well as a place to record the results. You will be amazed how specifically God answers your prayers!

Psalm 37:4 says, "Delight yourself in the Lord and He will give you the desires of your heart." Reflect and journal about what it means for you to "delight yourself in the Lord."

I am convinced that God wants to work powerfully in your life through answered prayer. He desires to meet your needs (Phil. 4:19) and give you direction every day of your life (Proverbs 3:5, 6)!

If you want to know God's perfect will for your life, ask Him for it. Remember, once you ask, you must be willing to wait for His timing, trust that He has it all in control, and obey what you believe He has told you. (If "knowing God's will" is something you are unsure of, be sure to take extra time to study verses in the Bible on that subject, or ask a pastor, parent, or local Christian bookstore for additional resources to help you understand it.)

TRY IT! APPLY IT!

This section, REQUESTS, will be one in which you write the most. Once you begin to talk to God about all of your needs, desires, and dreams, you'll need another five pages to talk to Him about your family and friends, as well as the concerns of the world (such as hunger, disease, peace, and politics).

In order to remember to be diligent to pray for those who have asked you to pray for them and for those you want to pray for daily, a PRAYER REQUEST LIST is an ideal way to be effective in intercessory prayer. Depending on your time and ability to concentrate, make your list as detailed as fits your personality.

Next, list all your family members by name and include a little phrase by each of their names. Next, you might list your personal plans for which you are seeking God's guidance. A page for those in need of physical or emotional healing is appropriate for any prayer list. Include on your list the government leaders who need safety, protection, and wisdom from God. Remember to pray for those who are without basic needs and pray for organizations helping meet their physical and spiritual needs. Add missionaries, pastors and others who impact lives to your REQUEST list.

You will be amazed at how your heart grows in concern and love for others as you pray daily for them.

After you have prayed through your daily REQUEST list, ask God to direct every aspect of your day—your plans, your words, your steps. (I don't recopy my list each day, but I do leave space to add to it.) Each day, add any new situations that need God's intervention.

Another wonderful idea is to pray scripture verses. For example, Colossians 1:9-12 is an excellent passage to pray for yourself and others on a daily basis.

I firmly believe that God wants us to ask Him for direction for our lives—now and for the future. James 4:2 says, "You do not have, because you do not ask God." It is very exciting—and faith building—to watch God answer your prayer, especially when you have been diligent to ask Him for His will and waited for His answer!

NOW, YOU TRY IT and, in faith, expect results!

LISTENING

The Lord confides in those who fear Him; He makes His covenant known to them. Psalm 25:14

The spiritual discipline of listening to God is one of continual growth for all Christians. It takes practice to hear God's voice! In fact, younger Christians may not feel confident in pursuing this discipline, but wise and biblical counsel from a pastor, bible study leader, and the Word of God will encourage you to develop a listening ear.

This section can be most difficult as you learn to discern whether God is speaking to you. Many Christians wonder if the thoughts they are thinking are simply their own. Even though some doubt may exist, quiet yourself before the Lord and record what you feel He is saying to you. "Be still, and know that I am God." (Ps. 46:10)

Listening to God is not meant to be magical or mystical. Hearing God's voice in the midst of our busy lives, emotional pain, or even temptation comes with practice and takes discernment. But if you are regularly reading the Bible, it won't be long before you know the Shepherd's voice. (John 10:4)

I am most prepared to hear God's voice when I purposely find a quiet place to talk to Him, then listen to His thoughts as I read the Bible, then think about the verses I've just read. In those moments, I ask God to reveal His thoughts and plans to me and then I wait to hear His voice confirm, correct and direct me. Every day, I underline or highlight verses that relate to my life situations.

You may also hear God's voice as He uses others—Christian friends, pastors, speakers, or books—to prompt your thinking, actions, and emotions. Ask God each day to give you His thoughts! Ask the Holy Spirit to help you hear God's voice.

TRY IT! APPLY IT!

Begin this section with a silent or written prayer, asking God to speak to you through His Holy Spirit. Be specific in asking about your needs and decisions, and ask if He has any direction for you. Be silent and attentive to the next thoughts that cross your mind.

Many times a Scripture verse will come to mind. Write it down, then look up the reference if you don't know where it is. Turn to that verse and read the other verses before and after it. Look for verses that have direct implication or application to the prayers you have previously prayed in your PRAISE, ADMIT, REQUESTS, and THANKS sections.

Very often I am encouraged, comforted, corrected, or directed by what has come to mind and what I have read. Once, concerned about a move, the passage in John 14 about God's peace came to my mind. I had been somewhat anxious about where we were going to live. When I came to verse 2, "I am going there to prepare a place for you," my heart jumped with excitement and I wrote the verse down in my LISTENING section. That afternoon, a gentleman whom I had never met called and asked if our family would house-sit for him for three months!

On another occasion, I felt that God was telling me to watch my driving. I wrote the phrase down in my LISTENING section . . . and two hours later I got a speeding ticket. I have taken my LISTEN-ING section more seriously from that moment on!

Many times in my LISTENING section I have received hope through the Word of God. Every day, I wait and watch and ask Him for those words of encouragement and direction for my life—and every day, I hear His voice.

God might call you by name or speak to you about doing something for someone. You may feel led to pray for another person whose needs He brings to your mind. The more time you spend listening to God, the easier it will be to both hear and know His voice. You may want to begin with only a few minutes of silent listening and then allow your time with him gradually to increase.

MY PARTNER PRAYER NOTEBOOK

The Tool: *My Partner Prayer Notebook*

Hours in prayer caused me to examine what was really happening when I prayed. What were the scriptural principles behind the results I was experiencing? What were the limits involved in asking of God? Who was privileged enough to receive God's listening ear? And how did the Word fit in so critically into one's time in prayer?

Answers came by simply following *My Partner's* format of

- *P*raising God for who He is
- *A*dmitting my sins to Him on a daily basis
- *R*equesting of Him and believing that He hears and answers
- *T*hanking God daily for everything

And by

- *L*istening to Him and not talking, but recording
- *M*essages from Him through my pastor's sermons
- *N*ew Testament readings (understanding God better through Jesus' life)
- *O*ld Testament readings (understanding God better through the history of the Jews)
- *P*roverbs to increase in wisdom.

My Part

Praise

The PRAISE section began each daily appointment as my personal praise prayers to God. At first, it was an awkward section. Knowing how to sing praises to God, but not knowing how to write them, led me to the book of Psalms for inspiration. From the psalmists I discovered so much about God's character—His unfailing love, His constant care, His surrounding presence, and His invincible might and awesome power. I also learned how to pray!

Through the words of praise in the psalms I learned to fear God, not be afraid of Him, to respect and reverence Him. There was every reason to fear God, not to mention a few of the benefits listed in Psalms 25, 31, 33, and 34: those who fear Him gain instruction, lack nothing, and receive great goodness; His eyes are on them; and encamping angels surround them, bringing deliverance.

Spending time in the psalms, especially those written by David, I learned *how* to express my love for God in writing. By reading of David's "heart after God" through his convictions, intensity, and passion for the living God, I was forced to examine my own heartfelt feelings toward Him. Could I say, "I love You, Lord," with emotion or with head knowledge alone? I so admired and emulated David's total heart after God that I gained a new strength and intensity in my own relationship with God by daily rewriting verses in the psalms until they became my own expressions.

The psalms became a pattern for my two-way conversations with God. I would rewrite five to seven psalms each day, choosing the words and verses that genuinely described my particular, current circumstances or emotions. Through those very verses, God began to speak back to me. Almost as if I felt His touch or heard a voice, I began to recognize a "word" from the Lord, *just for me.*

One February I was to share my testimony at eight high-school assemblies, five being public high schools. The students would be required to attend, which often created a resistance to hearing an adult talk about the dangers of drugs and alcohol, or especially the love of God. Intimidated, I feared that it would be like going in front of one thousand sharks. (When high schoolers don't agree with you, they'll let you know!)

I had just received a phone call from the person who was booking me and she said, "There is one more high school that wants you to speak. Would you come earlier on that morning?" I grimaced and agreed, thinking, *"Hmmm, okay, I'll do it, but this is going to be emotionally difficult for me to speak at one more public high school assembly."*

Later that morning, I opened the book of Psalms. I had read Psalm 88 the day before. So I began reading and rewriting the verses from Psalm 89. I wrote, "The heavens praise your wonders, O Lord, your faithfulness too, *in the assembly* . . . !" I stopped writing. God *knew* I was very concerned about my upcoming assembly presentations. He knew I lacked courage; He knew I was afraid. He wanted me to know I could trust Him to be faithful.

Every day I wait for God to speak to me through the book of Psalms. Every day I come expecting to hear Him. In *my* words, Psalm 5:3 says, "Lord, this morning, I bring my requests to You and I wait in expectation for Your answer." Why wait? Why expect? Because God wants to communicate with us daily. To wait on Him, to expect Him to answer our prayers is not wishful thinking or childish dreaming, but it is a fact about His character. He answers prayer! My personal prayers of praise express my feelings, fears, and hopes to God. And *without fail*, God responds daily by assuring me of *His* faithfulness and sovereignty.

Admit

The ADMIT section was another pleasant and unexpected surprise. What might have been a time of browbeating turned into a planned time of written accountability to God for sins of omission *and* commission, always ending in daily personal revival.

I began this section by praying scripture, which were my first written words of confession each morning:

Search me, O God, and know my heart;
test me and know my anxious thoughts.
See if there is any offensive way in me,
and lead me in the way everlasting. (Ps. 139:23-24)

While professing the words of Psalm 139:23-24, God's Holy Spirit revealed the areas of my life over the last twenty-four hours that needed to be cleaned up and forgiven! Even by the time I finished writing those verses, I instinctively knew what to confess to God as sin in my life—anger, pride, or jealousy—never did a day go by without discussing some vulnerable area of my life with God! I quickly learned that keeping short accounts with Him released fresh forgiveness and filled me with a purifying fire.

When I first began the discipline of daily confession in writing, I was the mother of a toddler. I rarely showed my anger in public, but when I was at home alone with my son, he got shaken and yelled at loudly. I let him know he made Mom mad. It seemed every day I had to talk to God about my uncontrollable anger. Unbelievably, I didn't sense God rebuking me with words such as, "You are terribly bad and sinful." No, the Holy Spirit nudged me, saying, "You don't want Jacob to hate you when he grows up, do you?"

I had experienced a "yelling home" as a child and learned

those same explosive habits. But now I had a choice to control those emotions. I could change or get professional help. I could choose to shut my mouth, count to ten, back up, or turn around. I could do any of those things—but would I commit to doing them? *I had not made the decision to change.* Out of genuine repentance, I asked God, with the help and power of the Holy Spirit, to change me. And daily, that part of me became new.

What also surfaced was a very jealous person who envied people who were prettier, smarter, skinnier, or funnier than me. I wanted to be their friend, but I wouldn't make an effort to get close to others because they were "better" than me.

One particular instance stood out. A dynamic young volunteer worker came to help in our ministry, but she unknowingly threatened me. She would make appointments with kids, and I would become angry with her, haughtily asking, "Why did you do that without my permission?" Though ashamed of myself, I could barely control my jealousy. I was embarrassed to admit it, but the bottom line was this: kids liked her, and I didn't want them to like her more than they liked me.

Eventually, she just "backed off" because I never gave her an opening to use her skills and gifts. When she moved away, without being able to have an effective ministry, my heart was terribly convicted. God showed me that I had squelched the opportunity of having a terrific addition to our staff because of the sin of jealousy. Yes, calling it sin instead of a bad habit quickly brought resolve. With true regret and humiliation, I purposed to turn from sin and sought counseling to control my inner thought life.

Some mornings, I would struggle longer in this section than in others. The words *integrity* and *holiness* were now a part of my personal agenda, not merely spiritual terms to describe the theologically oriented or seasoned Christian, but words I longed to see define my character.

The Holy Spirit began to gently direct me to Scripture, books, or conversations that would lead me to desire holiness. The seriousness of it all certainly didn't fit my personality or my previous track record of impulsive-compulsive behavior; therefore, I would leave the ADMIT section every morning by writing the words in my own paraphrase: "Transform my mind, please, God. Supernaturally fill me with Your Holy Spirit, overflowing. Cleanse me. Renew me. Change me." (Romans 12:1-2) It was a fact. The undisciplined person I had been all those years was obviously going to need a lot of transformation. Mother Teresa put it this way: "Our progress in holiness depends on God and ourselves; on God's grace and our will to be holy. We must have a real living determination to reach holiness."

In Luis Palau's book, *Heart After God*, he states,

> Nobody gets fat over night. Immorality begins with tiny things. Little things. Yet, if you don't crucify them, if you don't bring them to judgment, if you don't face up to them for what they are—sin—they can destroy you. They can blur your moral judgment at a critical, irreversible junction in your life. No one sees the little flaws. But everyone sees the big collapse.

Determined to be holy, for God's sake, and delighting in the freedom from guilt that comes from daily confession of sin, I genuinely looked forward to a time of daily revival in the ADMIT section of *My Partner Prayer Notebook*.

Requests

In the REQUESTS section, my faith was both stretched and made strong. In this type of prayer—*asking*—I discovered many principles that God Himself set forth in His Word.

Initially, I began with a two-page prayer list of people's names, followed by a phrase or two after each name that would specify my request for them (healings, interviews, tests, etc.) Praying for *others* created a deep concern and genuine interest in their lives.

In addition, on my list were upcoming events, financial situations, ideas needing further direction from God before pursuing, and request for God's advice on planning for the future.

Then the inevitable occurred.

Questions! Was I asking for too much, too often, over too many days? How long was long enough to pray for something? Was it God's will? Who was I to pray so boldly? Why did some requests take so long? Was God listening to me?

The next obvious step was to search the Scriptures, consider my own motives, and find out what other authors had to say about "requesting" prayers.

Over time and research, I learned that prayer was not just receiving "yes" answers to every prayer. As C. S. Lewis put it, "The essence of request, as distinct from compulsion, is that it may or may not be granted."

Psalm 37:4 says, "Delight yourself in the Lord and he will give you the desires of your heart." This verse encouraged me to ask of God because He truly does want to grant the desires of my heart. But it also exposed that my motives had to be taken into consideration before asking! Was I delighting in Him—spending time with Him—or just selfishly looking for God to make me happy?

The 16th verse in the book of James says, "The effective, fervent prayer of a righteous man avails much." (NKJV) This verse proved to be much like Psalm 84:11 which states, "No good thing does He withhold from those whose walk is blameless." As I applied those Scriptures to a prayer request list, it was essential to ask two questions during the interim time of waiting upon God's answers:

1. Is this a "no good" thing for which I'm asking? Is it in agreement with God's written Word, in accordance with the law of the land, and in keeping with personal integrity?

2. Has my "walk" been blameless? Am I making right choices? Are my words truthful? Do I slander others and do I keep my oaths (as suggested in Psalm 15 and Psalm 24)?

James 4:2-3 simply kept me asking in prayer; it challenged me to check my motives, and then cautioned me not to doubt, but trust in God's best provision—whether it be "yes" or "no."

What began as a simple prayer request list developed into a fifteen-page, exciting, on-going, faith-filled adventure with God!

Thanks

For the final section in MY PART of prayer each morning, I would handwrite a thank-You note to God. Simply put by O. Hallesby, "To give thanks means to give glory to God with our lives, with the wonderful things that happen and how He works within us."

Acknowledging God's sovereignty and intervention in every single area of our lives—feelings, finances, family, friends, and the future—is a daily reminder of our humanity and the need for His divine presence and intervention in our lives. Oh, we can get cynical, grumpy, lazy, or forgetful of all the good that God brings into our daily lives, but THANKS is to remember how often He forgives us and how carefully He delivers us from trouble. A thank-You note quickly ushers entitlement out of our lives and gives God the glory and honor due His name. Thanking God is not a mere check-off on the list of wants, but acknowledging His goodness and grace, expressed in writing by a grateful recipient.

God's Part

Listening

The LISTENING section of *My Partner* proved to stump me initially. It involved some risk. If I listened, would the God of the universe speak to me? I took seriously the directions for a rookie listener given by an older Christian: "Put your pencil to the paper then ask God, through His Holy Spirit, to speak to you. Write down what you feel He is saying to you."

Still not confident, I found more instruction in books by Andrew Murray, such as *The Prayer Life*, *Inner Life*, *Confession*, *Forgiveness*, and *Christ on the School of Prayer*. These books brought elusive spiritual disciplines into practical terms by discussing Murray's actual experiences of listening to God. They provided pastoral insights and numerous biblical references, blowing away much of the fogginess attached to listening to God.

As A. W. Tozer explained listening to God in *The Pursuit of God* it became more tangible:

> I think the average person's progression will be something like this. . . .
> First, a sound as a presence walking in the garden.
> Then a voice, more intelligible but still far from clear.
> Then the happy moment when the Spirit begins to illuminate the Scriptures and that which had only been a sound or at best a voice now becomes an intelligible word, warm and intimate and as clear as the word of a dear friend.

Listening to God was not intended to be magical or mystical or frightening. Our attitude should be to be in awe of God but not afraid of what He might say. Frankly, the greatest problem most of us have in listening to God is not obeying what we hear Him saying to us!

One day, I had stepped over the boundary of hearing and not doing. While writing in my LISTENING section, I simply wrote down the phrase, "Watch your driving." That phrase, not being particularly scriptural, caused me to consider it a rather unusual journal entry. Nonetheless, I had a distinct feeling that I would be challenged that day in the area of driving.

One hour later, I was pulled over by a policeman who proceeded to give me an expensive ticket for speeding! I got out of the car and stood on the side of the road as he finished writing up my ticket. He said, "Lady, get into your car. You're going to get hit!" I was shaking my head and crying in disbelief. I hadn't listened! God had told me to "watch my driving," and I hadn't listened.

Listening to God is a "must" for every believer. It is a discipline learned and developed through practice. Some of us have never tried it, while others listen to God regularly. If we would just plan time to listen and have a willing heart, He will meet us and speak to us. Psalm 25:14 promises, "The Lord confides in those who fear Him; He makes His covenant known to them."

Messages

The MESSAGES section of *My Partner* is the place to take notes of sermons and Bible studies in order not to miss or forget God's Word revealed at any given time. Approaching each convention, sermon, or weekly meeting with an attitude of openness toward change allows God's voice to be heard.

Recently our pastor was interviewing a fellow who tithed to his church before generating the income. I was scribbling down notes of the discussion when I literally looked up and thought, *Hey, I should try this, too!* Knowing our high-school ski camp was the following weekend, I decided to offer one scholarship if someone had the need. Upon leaving the church service, I bumped into the high-school intern and began to mention my desire to offer a ski trip scholarship. Two minutes later, a student joined in step with us. He couldn't afford to go to camp, but was there any other way? Absolutely!

I know of *numerous* times when my pastors have preached sermons that have inspired me to take gigantic steps of faith. The dream to write a book, detailing my life as a teenage alcoholic, became reality after listening to sermon after sermon by one of my pastors who was doing a series on believing in God's dreams for one's life. Not long after, my first book, *Just One Victory* rolled off the press! The outline for *My Partner Prayer Notebook* came after hearing a motivational Sunday morning message. A third sermon caused me to persevere during difficult times, doubling notebook distribution rather than completely stopping production.

I'm thoroughly convinced that God intends to speak to us through our spiritual leaders, and taking notes won't allow us to miss or forget what is said. Having pen and paper ready during a sermon causes concentration and encourages one to apply what is heard.

Hebrews 13:7 exhorts us to "remember your leaders, who spoke the word of God to you. Consider the outcome of their way of life and imitate their faith." Convention speakers, retreat and conference workshop leaders, spokespersons on Christian radio and television—all provide God's Word to the believer on a continuous basis. The Word of God, spoken through our leaders, has the power to send us out powerfully transformed and dramatically changed from the way we entered—if we are willing!

New Testament and Old Testament

Psalm 130:5 explains the way I've grown to view my Bible reading: "I wait for the Lord, my soul waits, and in His word I do hope" (NKJV).

Shortly after deciding to pray for one hour a day, I also decided to read through the Bible each year. By simply reading a version of a 365-day bible called the *Change Your Life Daily Bible* (a special edition of the One Year Bible®), I have read through the entire bible for over two decades. In so doing, both the New Testament and the Old Testament have been God's daily and constant source of encouragement, correction, direction, and comfort in my life.

But *boring*, *monotonous*, *exhausting*, and *irrelevant* are not words that describe my planned time in the Word. More descriptive words would be *life-changing*, *risky*, *adventurous*, *faith-stretching*, *comforting*, and *motivating*. When I was a young Christian, my mentor (and husband) advised me to daily read the Bible and not put it down until I heard God's voice.

How does that happen? I let the Word of God speak to my soul. From David's discourse in Psalm 119, I've learned to allow the Word to

- Keep me from sin (v. 11)
- Open my eyes to new and wonderful things (v. 18)
- Counsel me (v. 24)
- Strengthen me (v. 28)
- Give me understanding (v. 34)
- Direct my paths (v. 35)
- Turn my eyes from worthless things (v. 37)
- Be the theme of my song (v. 54)
- Teach me knowledge and good judgment (v. 66)
- Make me wiser than my enemies (v. 98)
- Keep my feet from every evil path (v. 101)

Psalm 19:11 says it concisely: "By them [the commands of

the Word] is your servant warned; in keeping them there is great reward."

I've found it essential to have a pen and a highlighter to accompany my Bible so that I can date and underline a Scripture passage of promise, direction, or hope. Seeing dates and references beside Bible verses is a powerful reminder of God's faithfulness. In fact, when tempted to doubt God's timing or to be discouraged, I'll peruse my Bible, just to remind me of His continuous intervention in my life.

One such time was on a ramp of the freeway. On the way to the Christmas Eve service, my tire popped and flattened—miles from the church. If that wasn't enough, the spare tire was combination locked beneath the rear of the van (and I forgot the combo!). Therefore, no tire, no jack, no option to fix was possible. Certain that the gas stations were closed for the holiday and any help was at church with my husband, I decided to go to a phone booth, and leave a message so that my husband could find me at the close of the service. We would sit tight until help arrived.

With at least an hour to wait, I opened my Bible to the book of Psalms and began to read familiar verses, wondering why I was sitting in a cold van and not a beautifully decorated, warm church! Some twenty minutes later I noticed Psalm 116:7 underlined with a date beside it: "Be at rest once more, O my soul, for the Lord has been good to you."

I smiled, thinking, Yes, God has been good to me . . . , and before I could finish the thought, my peripheral vision caught a shiny red one-ton pickup backing up to my vehicle. After I jumped out of my van and explained my dilemma, the young fellow proceeded to open his back hatch and pull out wire cutters and a hydraulic jack. Within fifteen minutes he had my tire changed and we were on our way to church!

Had this been the exception in my life, I would have passed

it off as coincidence, but God's Word was *continually* causing me to hope in Him then watch Him do incredible things everywhere I turned.

A young friend of mine, Jim Bennett, had a lifelong dream of becoming a big-league baseball player. During his last two years of college baseball, he also volunteered weekly in our high-school ministry. Soon, his dream became our dream! In his senior year of college, when the spring draft approached, we all prayed with great fervor for God's will in this matter. But God did not allow the door to open at that time. Somewhat disheartened, but still believing in Jim's dream, we continually prayed for an open door for him to enter the major leagues.

Almost two months had passed without a serious call from an interested club, yet we could not give up praying for a miracle. It was even difficult to talk about, almost like asking an overdue pregnant woman if she had had her baby yet, only creating more anxiety when the answer was repeatedly "no." Even as close friends began to give up hope, a few of us held on to the only fact left: we believed that God had put this dream in Jim's heart and we had to trust Him, somehow, to bring it to pass. One thing was certain. It would take God's intervention because the draft had ended over a month earlier.

One July morning in my quiet time, I read a Scripture verse that brought Jim to mind: "*Do good*, O Lord, to those who are good, to those who are upright in heart" (Ps. 125:4, emphasis added). I wrote Jim's name in my Bible and prayed, "Lord, He's so faithful to You and to the ministry with high schoolers, please . . . please . . ."

Feeling prompted by the Holy Spirit, I decided to call Jim. I found him at home, midmorning, probably waiting for a call—but not from me. I said, "Jim, I believe in your dream and that God is going to bring it to pass. I know how that waiting feels. I, too, have a dream that seems elusive. But, I read a verse this morning. I believe it's for you. Would you like to pray together and ask God to open a door this week?" Jim seemed excited and confident. We shared verses and prayed for each other's long-awaited dreams. That very night Jim Bennett was called—and signed—with the Seattle Mariners!

You just never know what time spent with God in His Word will bring. It's just too great a risk to miss even one day.

Proverbs

Daily reading in Proverbs—a verse or a chapter—always brings an "elbow's nudge" to a situation. As practical as advice can get for daily Christian living, the Proverbs always has a timely word for its reader.

For the procrastinator, Proverbs 24:33-34, "A little sleep, a little slumber . . . and poverty will come on you like a bandit," serves as a serious reminder to get up and get going! Everything from receiving wise counsel to guarding what comes out of your mouth (i.e., gossip or nagging) to warning against sexual immorality unfolds throughout the thirty-one chapters (making it convenient to read one chapter each day of the month)—reminding us that the instructions in the book of Proverbs still apply to today's believers.

The book of Proverbs is actually a relevant guide for living the Christian life. Chapter after chapter is filled with simple but solid advice.

Should I follow the crowd?	Read Proverbs 1.
Is morality outdated?	Read Proverbs 2.
How can I be wise?	Read Proverbs 3.
Affairs? Adultery?	Read Proverbs 4-7.
What's better than money?	Read Proverbs 8.
What's wrong with a little "fun"?	Read Proverbs 9-10.
What's the point of being proud?	Read Proverbs 11-12.

A quick temper?	Read Proverbs 13-15.
Plans? Decisions?	Read Proverbs 16.
What is the relationship between pride and the tongue?	Read Proverbs 17-19.
The price of procrastination ?	Read Proverbs 20-22.
Taking advice?	Read Proverbs 23-24.
What about honor and integrity?	Read Proverbs 25-27.
Accepting criticism?	Read Proverbs 28-29.
Advice for life?	Read Proverbs 30.
Signs of an exceptional woman?	Read Proverbs 31.

A proverb a day has a powerful way of influencing every area of your life!

To Do

Though TO DO was not in the acrostic of MY P.A.R.T. or GOD's PART of *My Partner Prayer Notebook*, ideas, thoughts, and reminders would pop into my head while praying and reading the Bible. Psalm 90:12, "Teach us to number our days, that we may gain a heart of wisdom" (NKJV), became a daily prayer as time with God continued to reveal just how important each hour of the day could be if used wisely for Him. I wanted desperately to be a good steward of my time, but I lacked certain disciplines. The need to organize my time became evident, and a TO DO list for each day was a must!

It has been interesting to watch how prayers turn into dreams and goals. Continuous prayer about specific goals becomes the motivation to live out these ideas and turn them into action steps on a TO DO list and calendar.

In fact, I had been given an idea in prayer for prayer that had radically changed my entire life. I was convinced, along with Peter Marshall, that "when I neglect to pray, mine is the loss."

Written prayer became my focal point.
  Recording God's answers,
    Pouring my heart out to God in writing, and
    praying through specific prayer request lists
      became a daily part of my life.

My Partner Prayer Notebook was the place for my daily appointment with God, the organizational tool that made it happen every day. The next, natural step was to make it available for many others to use.

Friends of *My Partner Prayer Notebook*

It was all systems go, and life was moving along like an Indiana Jones adventure—full of excitement, suspense, and the thrills of fighting and winning battles. Soon more and more adults and students wanted me to share about the power of prayer and the uniqueness of keeping a written record of your two-way conversations with God. Student ministries, churches, colleges, and other organizations began to request prayer workshops and seminars, and as a result, I received letters from many people—young and old—who were finding God to be real through their written conversations with Him. Everyone seemed excited to find an organized tool (similar to their personal calendar systems) for enhancing their daily time with God. But most rewarding and touching were letters from those whose lives had truly found release from guilt, courage to change, and revival in their personal relationship with God. They had stories they wanted to share as a result of their new decisions to write their prayers, and I've included a few of them here.

Birgette wrote from Paradise Valley:

*I began a study and prayer time based on your ideas. . . .
it's so exciting to see answers to prayer! If I hadn't written*

down the prayer requests I would not have been able to see God's hand at work!

Alice wrote from Illinois:

I accepted your challenge to spend at least an hour with the Lord every morning. This has been one of the greatest spiritual weeks of my life. The Lord has awakened me early every morning to keep my appointment with Him. . . . [The My Partner] formula for quiet time has helped me organize my devotional time and writing everything down keeps my thoughts on track.

Caryn wrote from Minnesota:

I am in a leadership training program. When I complete the program I will be able to counsel at camp. My instructor was reminding us of the importance of having a vital quiet time—so we could guide students and know what we were talking about when we told them about quiet times! At that point I realized that my quiet time was just something that had to be done every morning. Through your "program" my quiet time has become exciting.

Rebecca wrote from California:

After spending two years in a diminished relationship with God, I have been asking God to show me a way to get back on course with Him in an intimate, rather than superficial way. I have let my struggling marriage draw me away from God. I believe My Partner Prayer Notebook will truly help me to seek His kingdom (righteousness, peace and joy) once again in my life and cause a spiritual renewal.

Kristin wrote from Colorado:

I was feeling my quiet times were just kind of humdrum— the new notebook has just added a spark. (Plus you know how I like to be organized!) I'm making a new commitment to the Lord to get up earlier and have a "real" quiet time.... It's easy to have long quiet times on the weekend and I've found them getting too short during the week.

Janet wrote from California:

At the retreat you shared how you had started spending an hour a day in prayer. For some time and through different people, the Lord had talked to me about that and for short periods of time I would try. But there was never that commitment that endured with the passing of time. The Lord had me at that retreat to hear you share. It was as though this was the time to make a definite commitment and I did.

The idea of writing out my prayers really appealed to me. So often during prayer I would lose my train of thought, forget what I had prayed about or fall asleep. It didn't seem to matter what time it was or where I was or what position I was in. There is something about writing things down that overcomes most of those problems. . . .

Much has happened since I made that commitment. I have found myself in hotel rooms with non-Christian friends and somehow found a way to get my hour in. I have been on vacation and have gone back to work full-time. I have had my hour of prayer early in the morning and late at night. Because of working full-time, I had to stop teaching a women's Sunday school class and because of that found myself without my group of Christian support. That hour a day spent with the Lord has kept me grounded and focused and I pray on target. I have shared with many friends how blessed I have been writing out my prayers. And I have really come to realize that prayer is a conversation between me and my heavenly Father—time for me to speak to Him and for Him to speak to me through His Word.

Janet continued:

You made the comment that you didn't tell God . . . (as in demanding) . . . but you ask God for specific requests and that if they are God's will that He let you know. You also said that you ask forgiveness for sins in your daily life.
I have seen God answer prayers in my life in marvelous ways and yet it is so easy to forget or become so involved in daily problems and not look to God to take care of the situations. I think it is wonderful to write down these experiences even if they may seem so small so that if we need to be encouraged we can go back and read. On Thanksgiving Day . . . my husband and I started to write all the answers to prayers or blessings God has shown us. I would recommend the idea to everyone!

It is a simple fact. Some of us sincerely want to take positive steps in our prayer lives, but we need a little nudge—or possibly a proven resource—to help us remain accountable and organized when our nature or personality leans toward procrastination or disorganization. For those who fall into those categories, *My Partner Prayer Notebook* is an organized tool for making and keeping appointments with God and for recognizing and recording—in writing—the awesome, incredible, life-changing conversations one can have with the Lord, not to mention the power that is released when one prays!

PART IV

DELIGHTS, DESIRES, DREAMS

CHAPTER 8

POWERFUL PRAYER PRINCIPLES

My daily appointments with God were power-releasing, faith-producing times that kept me accountable to God. Each new day was like an adventure awaiting me.

Eventually I became curious about the patterns recurring in prayer, so I searched through a concordance for verses in the Bible that contained the words *ask*, *believe*, and *pray*. I discovered that prayer was an often unused, unbelievable power source! Some of the verses appeared too good to be true, almost challenging me to test their validity.

Having heard some of these verses discounted at previous periods in my Christian walk, I set forth my findings cautiously, though there was nothing cautious about them. Believing them as truth meant risky living—daring faith!

Over time, I gathered principles about prayer by observing Jesus' prayer life, applying His directives about prayer to actual circumstances, and imitating the way the New and Old Testament heroes talked with God. Though not an exhaustive list, six types of prayer became evident. Interwoven with the Word, the following patterns established biblical principles for personal prayer:

- Receiving prayer
- Believing prayer

- Revealing prayer
- Agreeing prayer
- Interceding prayer
- Persevering prayer

Receiving Prayer

Simply, but boldly, James 4:2 states, "You do not have, because you do not ask God." Taken literally, certainly we are encouraged to ask God, but James 4:3 continues with, "You do not receive, because you ask with wrong motives."

Therefore, a prerequisite of any request must be to ask of God. Don't *worry* about, *wish* to the stars for, or *demand* of Him what you want or need. But ask! Second, examine your motives, intentions or reasons for which you ask. Inquire of yourself honestly, "Is this request simply to spend on my own pleasure?" Both verses, if applied to daily life, become reasonable, scriptural guidelines for powerful and effective prayer!

In January 1988, I had to make a business decision about expanding or dissolving my three-year-old small business. I was faced with the challenge of needing $12,000 to move ahead or requiring no money to give up. Giving up seemed a lot easier, but I truly did not believe it was God's plan. Assuming a large loan seemed inappropriate, but it was an option. In my quiet time one morning, I got the idea to negotiate twelve monthly payments of $1,000—which seemed more manageable—yet still a bit unreachable. It was a saying by my pastor at the time that gave me a push in the right direction: "You don't have a money problem. You have an idea problem."

For two weeks every day, I prayed about where to get the initial capital. I knew (at least firmly hoped) that once I had the merchandise, it would generate the subsequent monthly payments. I just needed that first $1,000. Then I began to worry and fret. If this was God's idea, where was His provision?

As I was driving down my street toward home, the words of James 4:2-3 popped into my head, "You do not have, because you do not ask . . . " Let's see, I've worried and fretted over this, and I don't believe that the capital is for my pleasure, but for getting prayer notebooks into people's hands. Have I simply asked? After pondering that question, I could not say I had come right out and asked God for $1,000.

So, I did. I prayed, "Lord, would You give me $1,000 for the first monthly installment to buy prayer notebooks?" As I pushed my garage door opener and pulled into the driveway, my husband stuck his head out the door. He said, "Beck, your brother is on the phone." Having *just* prayed that prayer, I whispered to God, "Could this be an opportunity?"

Without delay, and probably little forewarning, I asked my older, single brother if he had $1,000 I could borrow for about one month. Without hesitation he said, "When do you need it?" I answered, "Tomorrow!"

Two weeks later, I paid my brother back in full with interest . . . and the rest is history!

Scriptures, including James 1:2-5, convince us that God wants us to *ask* Him about everything and He will not scold us for asking. He doesn't always answer "yes" or in the way we want Him to answer, but the Word clearly encourages believers to ask of God.

In Matthew 7:7-8, Jesus said, "Ask . . . seek . . . knock." He seemed to be saying, "Just don't sit idly and expect things to happen. Write a letter, do research, or even go door to door, and doors *will* open!"

A very well-known national author and speaker, Dr. Norman Vincent Peale, was coming to our church. Because of his inspiring life, a little time with him was probably worth a year of motivation for a young author. But how was I to get an appointment with him? I prayed *earnestly* for God to open a door.

Just ask, seek, knock, I kept thinking. It doesn't cost anything to ask and it will hurt only a *little* if he says, "No!" Anyway, not to ask for an appointment produced more anxiety.

At the suggestion of a friend, I dropped off a letter of request for an appointment at Dr. Peale's hotel and was delighted to receive a call scheduling an appointment with both Dr. *and* Mrs. Peale!

The fifteen-minute appointment turned into an hour and a half of ideas, encouragement, inspiration, and prayer. Near the end of our time together, I asked Dr. Peale for ideas on promoting personal prayer. He suggested that I write an article and submit it to a Christian magazine. He reminded me that people weren't going to always ask me to write for them, especially if they didn't know me or hadn't heard of me.

Upon returning home, I immediately sent a query letter to an editor of a Christian magazine, and believe it or not, I received an acceptance of a reprint of my first article on prayer. I thought, *"Hey, this principle is dynamic!"*

Receiving so many answers from God created additional questions about prayer. So many people believe that asking God about great concerns is acceptable, but to make insignificant requests to Him is inappropriate and bothersome. Searching the Word once again convinced me that He wants us to consult Him about everything. Who better is there to consult or discuss our concerns with than God?

Philippians 4:6 seemed direct encouragement to everyone who prays, "Don't worry about anything; instead, pray about everything" (TLB). The prayer premise became clear: (1) if God had exceptions, He would have listed them and (2) He would not have used the word everything if He hadn't meant everything. Therefore, to pray about *everything* should affect

- Personality struggles
- Finances
- Goals and dreams
- Trials
- Family relationships
- Purchases

- Friendships
- Vacations
- Emotional hurts

- Homes
- Lost items and contacts

The list goes on . . . and on . . . and on . . . and so does God's intervention.

In Philippians 4:6, the directive to pray about everything is preceded by, "Don't worry about anything." Just as in Matthew 6, Jesus had a better way for dealing with the realities of daily life, "Do not worry about your life. . . . Who of you by worrying can add a single hour to his life?" What was His advice in replacement of worry? "Seek first his kingdom and his righteousness, and all these things will be given to you as well. Therefore do not worry about tomorrow" (vv. 25, 27, 33-34).

The song of the year in 1988 ironically projected comical relief with its jazzy chorus, "Don't worry. . . . Be happy." But how can happiness practically be experienced in a believer's life?

I attempted to live the "do not be anxious about anything" theory while participating in a large youth convention. Every assignment given to me and every circumstance of the coming week created high levels of stress and anxiety *before* I had even stepped off the plane! I knew I needed a strategy for Spirit-filled convention living. I hadn't even unpacked when out of mental exhaustion I dropped to my knees beside the bed and cried, "O God, help me!" His presence was comforting; His thoughts came over me, "Get down to basics. Remember Philippians 4:6. Don't worry. Pray."

At that point, I made a conscious decision that whenever I experienced an overwhelming, dull feeling in my stomach or felt bombarded with too many stress-producing thoughts, I would simply pray. I'd admit my anxieties, release my worries, and request His ideas for handling the moment. In large or small situations I determined that *prayer, rather than worry* would be my strategy.

Within the first hour at my post, I recognized jealous and inadequate feelings bombarding my mind. I stopped them by praying for forgiveness (if I had dwelled on any of them) and requesting God's help in averting them. That lasted two minutes; they returned. I prayed again, vowing that I was not going to be anxious. They returned again; only it was ten minutes later this time. I repeated the pattern until I totally forgot I had a problem. Only later in bed that night did I even recall the situation.

Encouraged by my initial victory, and determined to go through each day without worrying, I found I constantly had to whisper Philippians 4:6 under my breath as a reminder of my goal. For example, frantically looking for people seemed ineffective on the large campus, but praying that I would find them brought them around the corner every time. Conversations seemed awkward to initiate, but when I prayed about it, the problem was resolved through seemingly coincidental remarks.

God was proving to me that a willingness to pray, rather than worry, unleashed His power to work and increased my trust in Him. It became evident that He was willing to bring His peace and patience into the minute or grand daily responsibilities and every relationship if I would just *pray*!

However, when a door does not open as hoped or prayed for, it is essential to believe, even amidst the disappointment or pain that God is still in control. As evidenced in Joseph's life and demonstrated in so many Christian biographies, *without fail*, though days, months, or years might pass, God can, He will and He does turn to good what seemed a loss or something meant for evil.

Believing Prayer

If the Scriptures weren't convincing enough in stating, "If you believe, you will receive whatever you ask for in prayer"

(Matt. 21:22), George Muller fueled my fire to pray, *believing*. A story about his prayer life became a constant reminder that it is not the impossible, the possibility, or the promise we are to believe in. We are to put our belief in the One who promises! We are trust in God's power, love, and faithfulness.

Norman Harrison in *His in a Life of Prayer* tells how Charles Inglis, while making the voyage to America a number of years ago, learned from the devout and godly captain of an experience which he had had but recently with George Muller of Bristol. It seems that they had encountered a very dense fog. Because of it the captain had remained on the bridge continuously for 24 hours when Mr. Muller came to him and said, "Captain I have come to tell you that I must be in Quebec on Saturday afternoon." When he was informed that it was impossible, he replied, "Very well, if the ship cannot take me, God will find some other way. I've never broken an engagement for 57 years. Let us go down to the chart room and pray." The Captain continued the story thus. "I looked at that man of God and thought to myself, 'what lunatic asylum could that man have come from?' I never heard such a thing as this. 'Mr. Muller,' I said, 'do you not know how dense the fog is?' 'No,' he replied, 'my eye is not on the density of the fog but on the Living God who controls every circumstance of my life.' He knelt down and prayed a simple prayer and when he finished I was going to pray but he put his hand on my shoulder and told me not to pray. 'Firstly,' he said, 'because you do not believe God will. And secondly, I believe God has. There is no need whatever for you to pray about it.' I looked at him and George Muller said, 'Captain, I have known my Lord for 57 years and there has never been a single day that I have failed to get an audience with the King. Get up and open the door and you will find that the fog has gone.' I got up and indeed the fog was gone. George Muller was in Quebec Saturday afternoon for his engagement. I learned from that man that if you know God and if you know His will for your life and circumstances seem impossible, pray believing that God will—and He will!"

I remembered that story when I was stranded in a California airport, unable to get to Tempe, Arizona, to lead a prayer workshop that noon. Upon hearing that the airport was shutting down for at least two hours, I panicked and called the party awaiting my arrival at the other end. The thought occurred to me that George Muller had faith to believe God would get him to his speaking destination, but I shrugged off the audacity of thinking that He might do the same for me, since I was no "George Muller."

Our connection was fuzzy as I tried to relay to the person who answered the phone that it looked like it would be over two hours before I'd be arriving at their airport, since some type of construction work had bottled up the runway. I suggested we pray, but reception between us was getting worse. I could barely hear her, but I knew she was praying for God's intervention. Thinking I had said, "Obstruction," rather than "construction," she prayed that God would remove the obstruction from the runway so that we could indeed meet on time for the prayer workshop. Hearing, "Amen," I told her I'd call when I had any news and hung up.

I picked up my pieces of luggage, slung them over my shoulders, and maneuvered my way back through the metal detectors to wait for any breaking news. No sooner had I gotten through the line and unload my luggage than a flight attendant came whizzing by me, commenting to a partner that the airport had opened. Disbelieving, I found an airport official to confirm the report and jockeyed my way back to the phone. Frantically searching for the phone number I had tucked away, I redialed and exclaimed the quick answer to prayer—there was no longer a delay.

As our plane was soaring across the state border I asked the gentleman next to me if he had any insight into why an airport would allow construction during a busy weekday morning.

He responded, "Lady, there was no construction problem. There was a bomb on the runway that, for some unknown reason, was removed impulsively by a county sheriff rather than wait for the bomb squad to arrive." My stomach turned!

It proved to be an incredible similarity of stories. At that afternoon's prayer workshop I read George Muller's account and relayed mine to the women. But even more unbelievable was the woman who had prayed for the "obstruction" to be removed, when I had told her it was a "construction" problem on the runway!

The "believing prayer" principle and George Muller's model of prayer caused me to constantly look for God to do the impossible, extraordinary, and unbelievable in my life. I likened my enthusiasm for prayer and the dynamics it created to the early Christians in the book of Acts—something always seemed ready to explode, erupt, or unloosen. Life *with* prayer was incredibly exciting and stretching in comparison to life *without* prayer.

The anticipation in the words of Habakkuk 1:5, I am going to do something in your days that you would not believe, even if you were told," caused me to hold on to that Scripture, over and over, until I memorized it and made it a part of my daily thoughts. It created an awareness to believe that God had plans in store for our lives that were exciting and unbelievable!

Being a dreamer, I always seemed to imagine grander scenarios of what God wanted to do with our church, our city, and

our ministry. But in September of 1985 when my husband submitted his resignation to the local board as Executive Director of
Youth for Christ, giving nine months' notice in which to find
and train a replacement for his position, I began to dream even
bigger!

A little apprehensive because we did not have our "marching orders" from the Lord for where we were to go next, we
prayed diligently that God would show us. Secretly I was praying for the some really exciting opportunity to take us somewhere special! I took hold of Habakkuk 1:5 and told my closest
friends that I believed God was going to do something we would
not even believe-something so exciting that in our own imaginations we couldn't even conceive it!

Things got a bit unnerving when my husband's replacement
was chosen in February, and we still had no "call." Then, as circumstances unfolded, on one weekend we were offered two
jobs, one in Florida with Youth for Christ and one in California
at a large church.

Because we wanted *God's* will for our lives, it was, in fact,
the verse in Habakkuk that showed us which way to go. In each
of the options where we could move, and the possible combi-
nations of what we could do as a ministry team, in our wildest
imaginations, we had never considered working together in a
large California church, even though we had visited and loved
California. Being from Cleveland, Ohio, it just seemed too good
to be true. But God was opening a door that was "exceedingly
abundantly above all that we [could] ask or think" (Eph. 3:20,
NKJV). We made the leap, sold everything we owned, and moved
all the way across the country!

Believing prayer has many facets to it. It has received unfair
billing by some people as "prosperity blessing" teaching. But
when applied biblically it is the foundation of faith: "*Without
faith* it is *impossible* to please God, because anyone who comes

to him *must believe* that he exists and that he rewards *those who earnestly seek him*" (Heb. 11:6, emphasis added).

Oh, to believe God for the impossible in our lives—not because we deserve it but because He is awesome and powerful—and to allow Him to be glorified in the results is an extremely challenging, but powerful, prayer principle for those who believe!

Revealing Prayer

James 1:2-6 says, "Don't be afraid to ask of God. He will not scold you if you don't know. . . . but don't doubt His will, once He reveals it to you" (author's paraphrase).

This Scripture is a helpful principle used for determining God's will for *any* given situation. Having a "feeling" about a request, one way or another, but not sensing God's affirmation or confirmation through Scripture and His Spirit, prompts simple questions, "What is Your will, God? How would You have me to pray?"

What is a revealing prayer? Rather than trying to convince God of something, ask Him to convince you of His will. Ask Him to give you a sense of His assurance through (1) Scripture, (2) the Holy Spirit's impression upon you, and (3) the godly counsel of other Christians. Then wait for Him to bring the answer. Having no time limits, this principle can unfold over a day or a month or even a year.

One of my first "revealing prayers" occurred after attending C.L.A.S.S. (Christian Leaders and Speakers Seminars) not far from home in Columbus, Ohio. The goal of C.L.A.S.S. was to teach men and women methods for teaching and sharing their testimonies in an organized and dynamic way. When they mentioned further training, I felt that I was on the threshold of something exciting and my heart burned with desire to go to the ADVANCED C.L.A.S.S. where attendees would be taught even more techniques in public speaking. There was only one problem. It was in southern California, which meant I had to get approval from Roger, my husband, and find money in our checkbook. Being on a parachurch ministry staff, we didn't have a monthly income that provided for gallivanting across the country, especially without advance notice or planning.

Nonetheless, I felt convinced that God wanted me to go. So I brought the subject up as soon as I got home. But Roger, having been the at-home-parent for the previous weekend said, "Becky, I give an inch and you take a mile."

"But, Rog, I believe God wants me to go!" I prayed continuously about it, my desires only growing stronger. Then one night in bed, I asked Roger to reconsider. I said, "Dear, what would it take for you to believe God wants me to go to ADVANCED C.L.A.S.S.?" Without much delay, Roger replied, "He'd have to pay your way."

Roger didn't make things really easy for me. But I continued to pray fervently and read verses that encouraged me, rather than discouraged me from asking God to let me go to California and to pay my way!

While sitting outside on the thirteenth day, having my quiet time, I had the distinct thought, "*Today is the day you'll know!*" I actually looked up into the sky and said aloud, "Did You say that, or did I say that?" Matter-of-factly, I decided God must be telling me "today" He would show us His will. I looked for His answer everywhere—in both my mailboxes and in every phone call. By eight o'clock that evening I walked past the telephone and whispered, "Okay. I thought I'd know today. Did I listen wrong? Did You tell me I'd know today, or was I hearing things?"

At 8:30 pm, the phone rang. It was Fred Littauer, calling from C.L.A.S.S. in southern California. He said we'd not met but he had a note that I was interested in ADVANCED

C.L.A.S.S. How could he help?

Little did he know I needed a lot of help—to the tune of about five hundred dollars. Without letting him know my dilemma, I asked about any payment plans or options for attending the seminar. He suggested using a credit card or prepaying in full. Well, that kind of closed the case, but we continued to chat regarding current speaking and writing opportunities. As I hung up the phone, I thought to myself, *"Well, I guess I did find out today!"*

Ten minutes later the telephone rang. "Becky, this is Fred Littauer again. God has impressed upon my heart to offer you a scholarship to ADVANCED C.L.A.S.S. in California this June!"

Much later I found out there had never been such an offer before or since that date in time. And it was sure fun in the Tirabassi home that night!

In addition, because of the initial contacts made with a woman at ADVANCED C.L.A.S.S. (later to become a dear friend), my husband and I heard of a job opening at her church and one year later we were hired to direct the youth ministry there!

It has become my practice, without fear of being laughed at by others or scolded by God, to ask Him how I should pray when I am unsure of His will. When He, in His many intricate and intimate ways reveals His will, my step in the "revealing prayer" principle is to *believe without doubting*, no matter how long it takes until I receive His promise.

God says, "Call to Me and I will answer you and show you great and mighty things which you do not know" (Jer. 33:3, NKJV). God is saying, "Just ask. It's no secret."

Interceding Prayer

The purpose of the request section of a prayer notebook to

gather and pray over a specific list of the needs and desires of family, friends, coworkers, organizations, politicians and those we may not even know.

In praying for others, we receive a model for intercession from both Jesus and Paul. Jesus Himself prayed often for His disciples, and Paul verbalized in the beginning of many of the New Testament letters not only *that* he prayed for the saints, but *how* he prayed for them.

In Philippians 1, Paul says that

- He thanks God for the believers (v. 3).
- He feels joy because of their partnership in the gospel (v. 4).
- He prays that their knowledge of God will grow deeper, so they will grow blameless until the day of Christ (v. 9).

In Colossians, Paul lists in detail how he prays for the believers, saying that he has not ceased praying for them and asking God that they be filled with the knowledge of God's will, live a life worthy of the Lord, and bear fruit (Col. 1:9-12).

Making it a practice to pray for every single family member by name each day, lifting (as Paul suggests) their spiritual needs up to God as well as their personal needs, large or small, is the core of intercessory prayer.

One particularly small request that I prayed daily was for my son, Jacob, when he was nine years old. He had a falling out with a friend. Neither of us could understand the situation, and though we tried, there never was complete reconciliation. Trying to trust God when the friendship did not rekindle, I asked Him if He would bring another friend along for Jacob. I guess the mother's heart hurt more than her son's, for he seemed to handle the indifference—and rejection—much better than Mom did! In addition, I prayed for Jake's personality to become more godly, knowing it takes two to create a solid friendship.

Almost eight weeks later, a little boy, whom he had known for the whole sports season, "all of a sudden" became his best little buddy. To top it off, both dads loved to fish and planned to take the boys out on the ocean. God had given both Jake and his dad new friends. And as if God wanted the last word, to quiet a mother's heart, Jacob's report card came home that semester with the comment, "Jacob is a well-liked student and has a super personality!"

Another small incident was in relationship to my parents. After being married forty-five years, couples can grow apart in interests. Hoping that my parents could enjoy their later years in life, I began to pray for my mom and dad's friendship. Just about three months later, my brother called. In the course of our conversation, Rick mentioned that Mom and Dad went out to breakfast almost every morning on their way to work. With an inner smile, I felt indirectly responsible for their "breakfast dates," especially since in all our growing-up years it was a rare occasion to eat out.

It's really interesting to pray for something to happen in the life of someone else and then watch it happen.

One friend had a definite response whenever I'd ask her to pray aloud—"no!" I asked her for two years, almost every time we ate lunch together, if she would like to say a prayer. She had not prayed aloud since she was a child, she related. Then I put that special request under her name on my list. One month later, in my home, I asked her if she would like to pray aloud with me. Hesitantly, she did, and it was a beautiful start to a regular time in prayer together.

On my personal prayer request list, I've added prayers for others who needed physical and emotional healing. Many people I meet and love struggle with addiction. I pray specifically that God would keep them from temptation and strengthen them; changing, even removing their unholy passions. Intercessory prayer is a powerful and tangible way to be involved in others' recovery. If we believe that prayer makes a difference in the lives of others, it is essential to commit time and effort in prayer for them on a daily basis.

One such time, a former Campus Life student of mine called our home. Though we hadn't seen him since he had been in our Campus Life club during high school, we had heard that his relationship with God had really suffered in college. Daily prayers were said for him (*for years*) to come back to the Lord. In his senior year of college, Jeff called one night to tell us that a fraternity brother, for over one year had not stopped inviting him to a bible study. He called to tell us he finally gave in, attended the study and recommitted his life to Christ. As the saying goes, "the hound of heaven" reached him, and since his initial telephone call, letters arrived requesting our support as he entered full-time ministry!

Intercessory prayers include praying for family and friends who have had cancer and other illnesses. Telling those who are ill that you are praying for them daily can be a true source of hope and encouragement for them. Praying for healing will absolutely stretch your faith and challenge you to seriously examine what the Bible says and what you believe.

When told of a friend's recent bout with cancer, we prayed that God would *reduce* the tumor. Many people were praying for her and believing with her for God's healing. She and I hadn't talked for almost three months when I saw her at a meeting. Though cancer is awkward to talk about, I wanted her to know I was praying for her, so I told her I was daily asking God to shrink her tumor. She looked at me, and with a smile, related that her doctor had recently told her the tumor had shrunk over 50 percent!

Not every person who asks God for healing is physically or immediately healed. But just as Jesus healed when He walked on earth, as detailed over and over in the Gospels, the documented testimonies that exist today conclude that He still heals! And though we may not understand all there is to know about healing, praying for God's healing when someone requires it does not appear to be outside His will or to violate scriptural teachings. Therefore, the principle is to *ask God how to pray* for someone, pray fervently in that way, and *trust Him for the results*.

Interceding becomes an act of faith that any believer can perform for any person anywhere in the world. Paul urges, "Devote yourselves to prayer" (Col. 4:2), and he challenges us to wrestle in prayer for others, to "stand firm in all the will of God, mature and fully assured" (Col. 4:12).

Agreeing Prayer

My dear prayer partner, Kinney, was unable for many years to have children. Those who can bear children usually don't fully understand the emotional pain involved in being barren. But no matter the situation, friends can share the anguish of others in their disappointments and hurts.

In October, after attending the youth worker convention together, Kinney and I attended a women's retreat. It seemed to come at a perfect time, lifting her spirits after a recent adoption fell through very late in the procedure which had caused her much despair. Not having many answers and little comfort over the weekend, we decided to visit the prayer room.

If Kinney and I had been close friends one year earlier, we probably wouldn't have felt that strongly about the power of prayer. But for the previous eight months, we had been on a wild chase, uncovering new truths about prayer as two young women finally getting serious about the serious things of God.

As we walked into the empty room I pondered how this was my first visit to a prayer room in my entire life. Compelled to kneel by two chairs, we prayed for almost forty-five minutes over the situation at hand: the inability to have children (though every conceivable test and operation had been attempted), the terribly disappointing adoption proceeding, and now, perhaps even worse, a loss of hope. We prayed. We cried and with tremblingly, we asked God to bring her a baby. We prayed scripture, allowing Matthew 18:19 to serve as a reminder "that if two of you agree on earth concerning anything that they ask, it will be done for them by My Father in heaven" (NKJV).

That night, during a concert, a woman neither of us knew tapped Kinney on the shoulder and said, "I understand you are looking for a baby." We slowly looked at each other in both awe and amazement! The incredible account *over the next six weeks* included an interview, more prayer, lots of applications, renewed hope, and the adoption of a beautiful baby girl named Ginny! The story of Kinney's Ginny is perhaps the most dramatic account of agreeing prayer that has occurred in my life. But on a weekly basis, it has become my practice to sit with family, friends, and staff members at spontaneous and planned moments and lift great and small needs to God in prayer, agreeing upon them in Jesus' name and leaving the incredible results up to Him.

On many occasions, urgent requests will cause praying over the phone with a prayer partner. Because time and miles don't allow us to be together, we'll pray believing that our pressing needs will indeed be heard by God. How exciting to call back after God responds to agreeing prayer and shout, *"You won't believe it!"*

On one occasion, I hadn't heard back from a person for over one month regarding a proposal I had submitted to his company. Praying daily about the response, but hearing nothing from the firm caused me to doubt the outcome. Not wanting to contact the company but needing some ray of hope to continue praying, I called my prayer friend, Marita, in San Diego and asked, "Will you pray for me and have your dad pray, too, that they would just let me know something by January 10?" "Of course," she replied.

My confidence was strengthened through her quick response to me. In addition to the Scriptures I had read in that morning's regular planned bible reading, I had been also been reading a book called *George Muller of Bristol*, the biography of his life of prayer. When I ran across this poem, my spirit soared:

> I believe God answers prayer,
> Answers always, everywhere;
> I may cast my anxious care,
> Burdens I could never bear,
> On the God who heareth prayer.
> Never need my soul despair
> Since He bids me boldly dare
> To the secret place repair,
> There to prove He answers prayer.

Next to the poem, in ink, I inscribed my prayer request and the date, January 9.

On January 10 the company's secretary called me. With a little twinge of excitement, I asked her if they had heard anything about my proposal. No. In fact, the person who would know was out of the office.

When we hung up, I pondered the thought, *"Well, Becky, you asked to know something by the tenth and at least you know that you can't know until next week! That's something . . ."*

When the phone rang that same afternoon and my friend from the company said, "Hello," I must have sounded confused by saying, "Why did you call?" He replied, "Why not?"

"You're right," I said. "I asked God if He would have you call today! And He did!"

I was able to discuss the proposal and gain enough hope to continue praying for favor with this company . . . and I almost blew the phone off the hook in San Diego when Marita's secretary answered and I screamed, "He called. God had him call!"

Agreeing prayer can become contagious when others around you see God's hand moving in incredible, sometimes seemingly impossible situations. One such time was when a couple on my volunteer staff, young in age and in spiritual growth, was really starting to move toward God with a more mature, renewed faith. They were engaged to be married and had been dating for two years, but their faith was now truly a part of their relationship (which had not been the case when they initially planned to get married). Shortly before the wedding they attended a church "College and Career Night" at a park to play volleyball. In the course of the evening, the young woman lost her engagement ring somewhere. It was not until she got home late that night that she realized it was even missing.

Frantic and concerned about the ring, she called her fiancé, and they searched everywhere . . . their cars, all the rooms she might have entered. But they could not find the ring. There was only one place left to look—the public park. They prayed fervently and asked God to help them find the ring.

The next morning they got up at five o'clock and went to the park before going to work. Not even knowing where to begin, they walked over to the volleyball court where the bride-to-be had been standing the previous evening. Looking down on the court, they saw a shiny gem. They immediately found her engagement ring! The fact that they had prayed together and God answered them so quickly in a seemingly impossible situation brought a new level of expectation and trust in their relationship with God and each other. Though the situation seemed negative at first, through answered prayer, they truly sensed God's intimate love expressed toward them.

From large to small agreeing prayers, God continually shows us that He is listening and faithful and that the size of the request is insignificant. For example, one morning, before speaking at a large women's event, my husband prayed very specifically for me. When I returned home early that afternoon, my husband asked me how the morning had gone. I related a wonderful story about meeting new friends and seeing old faces at the meeting. As I shared every detail, his smile grew bigger and bigger. He said, "I prayed for every one of those things to happen in your life today." Not only did I experience God's faithfulness in that situation, but my heart was really warmed to think that my husband agreed with me in prayer over what may seem insignificant to others but was important to me that day.

Praying with others for God's intervention in any given situation creates excitement and incentive to keep agreeing in prayer! Lost items, potential job opportunities, hopeful marriage partners, finances, the mending of relationships—from details to dreams—agreeing prayer is a faith-building experience not to be neglected.

Persevering Prayer

Andrew Murray, through his written works has become a prayer mentor to many people. In the early 1900s, as a minister in South Africa, he attended a conference that changed the path of his life with the Lord. The written stories of the revival that took place in Andrew Murray's heart and other's lives regarding the "sin of prayerlessness" read like a map, charting a course from self-examination and renewal to a deep dedication to daily appointments with God for any who would follow. As I uncovered more and more of his writings, I found his books on prayer were often discounted up to 75 percent off at bookstores, illuminating the fact that there are seasons when Christians are not really "into" prayer. Andrew Murray had written volumes on the power of prayer, but when I discovered them, they were tucked away on back room bottom shelves. Yet by reading and rereading certain chapters, I gained incredible insight and hunger for the power released by prayer. One such principle he would expound upon regularly was *persevering prayer.*

He said the secret of perseverance was "patience and faith, waiting and hasting." Murray taught that oft-repeated prayer was not wrong or un-scriptural. In Luke 18:1-8, Jesus told a parable to His disciples "to show them that they should always pray and not give up." The parable detailed a woman pleading before a judge for justice and mercy. He compared that story to God's children pleading to Him for justice and He assured the disciples that God's response would be even more merciful. In fact, in another conversation with the disciples on the subject of prayer, Jesus related a story of a man who received an answer to his requests *because* of his boldness and persistence.

There was once a young boy born in 1805 who had lived as a thief, a drunkard, and a liar. He was considered wicked beyond belief. Yet in his manhood he became admired as a beloved family man and respected pillar of the Christian community in England. He was said to have a motto for his life: prayer was the cornerstone with which his life's work was built. He had complete dependence on God and utter belief in the Bible. His work among the orphaned poor was divinely ordained. He prayed for direct divine guidance in every crisis, great or small, and the thread woven through his life was prevailing prayer. He undertook the building of orphanages strictly by means of faith. He never asked people for money; he only asked God. He found that any and all the needs of the work were always given and never once came too late. He found that even delayed answers to prayer served a purpose. It was said that over one million pounds were received during the years in which the evangelist George Muller built orphanages and maintained the care of hundreds of orphans. He stressed the importance in discerning the will of God before undertaking anything, but he said, "If our trust in the Lord is real, help will surely come." He received thousands of answers to prayer, even though he waited between twenty-nine and sixty years for certain answers!

His examples of persevering prayer saw me through a delicate and difficult matter. Unusual circumstances allowed me to say nothing and to be the recipient of little help, causing intense feelings of anguish and helplessness.

Every single day I would pray and ask God for relief from the seemingly unjust situation. And when there was no outside answer, a search of Scriptures would be the reminder that "God knows," developing a deeper hope in His deliverance than I had the day before.

Exactly three years later, to the day, the issue was completely removed from my life as abruptly as it had entered and without injury to me or my family. As I look back over those days of being barraged with doubt and fear, the Word of God and persevering prayer were my only and greatest strength. I can also acknowledge faith is greatly challenged to grow during trials. Yet when prayer becomes the avenue of daily releasing the anxieties of humanly irreversible situations to God and sensing His presence amidst the unknown, you have reached a new level of faith. At that juncture, the words of Hebrews 11:1 take hold and become real to us, "Now faith is being sure of what we hope for and cer tain of what we do not see." When we have preserved in prayer, these words no longer seem like vague words of theology; *they become our stronghold* in times of weakness, trail and testing.

The principle of persevering prayer soon became the foundation of many mounds of miracles yet to come in my life.

CHAPTER 9

MOUNDS OF MIRACLES

The sheer thrill of moving from the cloudy days, flat terrain, and cold, cold winters of the Midwest to the year-round sunny, warm days of southern California seemed too good to be true! But when reality struck, six weeks was an unbelievably short period of time to sell our house and cars, tie up loose ends, and get in as much time with family and friends as possible—not to mention taking forty-eight high school students on a "Florida Breakaway" in the midst of a move.

Perhaps all those reasons prodded me to ask the Lord for something special. It took us two of the six available weeks just to get our house ready for market--painting and even putting up new drapes—so when it actually came to listing and selling our home, acquiring a realtor seemed out of the question, unless someone was to stay behind or leave an outsider with the burden of selling an empty house and taking care of all the many details of a house sale. So I simply asked, "Lord, would You sell our house in a day?"

I had been reading in the book of Isaiah during the months prior to the big turn of events in our lives, and the chapters were full of promises and promptings to dream and soar and "not be afraid." I put my hope in these verses while still waiting for God's plan to unfold.

In chapters 40—60 of Isaiah, I constantly highlighted and dated verses related to being a messenger of the gospel. As hope gained a foothold in me and firmly believing that it was indeed God's will for us to move to California, I felt it was both bold and safe to at least ask for His supernatural intervention.

On Tuesday, I called the newspaper to place a "House for Sale" ad, giving all the details. The telephone solicitor asked if we'd be having an open house—a one-day showing. I said, "No." She continued to push me, oddly, until I agreed to show our home that coming Sunday from 1:00 to 5:00 P.M.—the "norm" she suggested for an open house.

Then I began to ask my friends to pray, "Would you pray with me and ask God to sell my house in a day?" Some jumped on the bandwagon with great anticipation, and others warned me by saying, "Well, you know, Becky, God doesn't always do things like that a second time."

Five years earlier, we had outgrown our little home after the birth of our son. With the same inkling that God was prompting me, I felt we should put our first little house up for sale on the Fourth of July (not a real hot day for house sales) with a specific, nonnegotiable selling price and without the assistance of a realtor. I believed God wanted our house up for sale that day! When I suggested this to my husband, he thought I was being a bit impulsive, but with his permission, that morning I hammered a big FOR SALE sign into our front lawn. Unbelievably we had a buyer for our full asking price that afternoon. Therefore, when a few of my friends didn't seem to believe God would answer that prayer, like George Muller's story about the captain, I asked them not to pray at all, because I believed God had been giving me Scriptures and an inner confidence—or faith—to believe that He certainly could sell our house in a day if He so desired.

That Sunday morning, I went forward to the altar for prayer after the service, again to solicit prayer for our one-day sale. It seemed ironic that even as the praying "shepherd" anointed me with oil and proceeded to pray for me, he seemed not to pray believing God would, but only that my faith would continue to be strong!

At 1:00 P.M. many visitors streamed through our doors, but by 3:00 P.M. not one person had placed a bid on the house or expressed a serious interest in buying it. At that point, my husband went to the car wash, and my son "bailed" on me and went to Grampa and Grandma's house down the street!

Alone in my family room, I looked up at God, then down at my Bible, and sincerely asked, "Did I hear You wrong or did You tell me that You would sell my house in a day?" Opening to Isaiah, I read, verse after verse, hoping for a glimpse or sign of His word to me. Then Isaiah 51:5 stood out on the page as if it were one-fourth inch higher than all the other verses: "My righteousness draws near speedily; my salvation is on the way." "That's it," I said aloud, closing my Bible. He did tell me. And whoever is going to buy this house is on the way!

The doorbell rang and a prospective couple entered. Before I could even start showing them the house, another couple entered the front door. Fortunately, my husband had returned and was coming in the door behind them.

One hour earlier, the second couple had been headed south on the highway. Picking up the newspaper, they ran across our open house ad and made an unplanned turnaround. By five o'clock that afternoon the "sale by owner" papers were signed, and the rest is history!

Almost as soon as the excitement of our Ohio sold-in-one-day house had erupted, the pressure of purchasing a new house in California intensified. We seemed helpless to be able to make arrangements, since the first day we landed in California would be our first day of work in one place and the last day of work at another. Timing, as usual, was *tight!*

My anxieties were soaring, having sold the last of our securities—home and cars—without replacements for them! Catching myself out of sync with the principles of prayer, I knew I needed to regroup and release God's power into our situation. I was reminded in Philippians 4:6-7 to pray about *everything* and not worry about *anything!*

Soon, a California realtor began to call with options of houses to rent for temporary relocation, but every time, certain details caused me to question his suggestions. I had grown accustomed to desiring God's best in any given situation, and each possibility seemed either too far, too much, or too risky. Some compromise always rose to the surface.

Knowing that my conditions were beginning to wear the realtor down, I finally accepted an offer, so as not to take his kind assistance for granted. But even as I hung up the telephone with him that morning, I talked to God, "Could this *really* be the best place for us? You have done so many amazing things, Lord, to move us from Ohio to California. Do You desire us to take this high-priced, far-from-the-church home?" A verse popped into my head: "My peace I give to you; not as the world gives . . . " (NKJV). *"Of course,:* I thought, *"I need Your peace."*

Wanting desperately for God to speak to me regarding this situation, not knowing exactly where that verse was found, I sat down at the kitchen table to read my Bible. I began in John, chapter 14, only to read these words: "Do not let your hearts be troubled. Trust in God; trust also in me. In my Father's house are many rooms; if it were not so, I would have told you. *I am going there to prepare a place for you*" (w. 1–2, emphasis added). I closed my Bible and thought, *"He is going there to prepare a place for me."*

That very morning the women's Bible study group at the new church we were going to work for discussed the fact that the youth pastor and his family were in need of temporary housing for the summer—asking if there were there any availabilities? A Bible study attendee, Clara Landrus and her husband trekked to Idaho each summer to help on their son's dairy farm. Hearing the need, she mentioned it to her husband at lunch, and he called our home that very afternoon!

Upon his introducing himself to me and offering his home—*free of rent*—I exclaimed, "He did it!" Jesus had gone before us that day to prepare a place for us. What a wonderful and warm start we had as Californians!

And with that same dogged determination I drove another realtor crazy until there was only one week in which to buy a home, allowing for the appropriate number of days for "closing" and "escrow" before Will and Clara would arrive home from their summer trip.

Now on our own, my husband noticed a little realtor's office next to a dry cleaner. He wanted to go in; I wanted to cry. Housing in California was incredibly expensive, higher than we had originally thought! Disillusioned with the choices available, in comparison to our nice roomy Ohio home, we realized it was going to take twice the money to buy half the home.

Daily, I prayed for a miracle, an open door, the right house for us . . . to no avail. Almost desperate, Roger convinced me this might be our last week to find a home; otherwise, we would need to move to an apartment and keep looking. I couldn't face another move, so I agreed to talk with another realtor. Even though he was friendly, I was not very responsive to his pitch.

Finally I said, "I've been praying a lot about our future home," then added we had only so much money and one week left to buy a home. He gave us rather confident smile, though he knew we were asking for a miracle. He, too, was a Christian; therefore, we closed our discussion with prayer, asking for God's special intervention—to show us the way to go!

Though he and my husband had looked at a few houses during the week, the first house they showed me that next Saturday became our little home, with all the desires of my heart included! And, appropriately, the move-in date was two days before the Landrus' were to arrive home. The selling realtor found these coincidences beyond explanation and, thinking I had connections with my well-known pastor, he said, "Hey, you must have had help from the big guy." I laughed, "Our help came from the Bigger Guy!" He laughed, too. The timing, once again, stretched us to persevere in prayer for God's best, reminding us of His perfect, intimate plan for our daily lives (Heb. 10:35-36).

Daily prayer became the opportunity to communicate to God our needs, hopes, and desires, asking for His best, and waiting and watching for His will to unfold—always beyond our expectations and always in *His* time frame. Oh, how perseverance develops faith!

In addition to each miracle that would cause me to hope in God whenever I was discouraged or impatient, the book of Psalms became my pattern for waiting upon Him. No matter the request—personal, emotional, financial, or relational—I learned to ask Him for daily deliverance and trust in Him *because* of His previously proven character. Verse after verse reminded me to "appeal [to] the years of the right hand of the Most High . . . [to] remember the deeds of the Lord . . . and [His] miracles of long ago . . . [to] meditate on all [His] works and consider all [His] mighty deeds."

CHAPTER

10

OPEN DOORS, ONWARD DREAMS

I became convinced that meeting with God for an hour a day was the best place to receive new ideas, goals, and dreams. As encouraged by Psalm 119, I used the Word of God as my counselor and path lighter and I allowed prayer to be my soul's expressions to Him. Receiving an idea from God and then watching it explode into reality was incredibly exciting and encouraging. But hindsight usually was more impressive than trudging through the steps of a dream, one day at a time, especially when others didn't have the same enthusiasm or when help was not on the horizon. Perhaps that is just where God would have us, dependent on His deliverance and helpless within our own strength, allowing Him to become strong when we are weak and to receive the glory for miraculous answers to prayer?

One such prayer idea that progressed from the dream stage to reality was *My Partner Prayer Notebook.*

It was no secret that many people struggled with having a consistent appointment with God. And I was certain that written accounts of God's intervention, assistance, and deliverance could be the catalyst for helping others not only make a daily appointment with God, but keep it. With that knowledge, I began to produce notebooks in bulk when my impetuous nature and interested users couldn't wait for someone else to develop an organized tool for written prayer!

But in the harsh world of business, the creation, publication, sales and distribution of an unproven product was not worth anyone's time except my own! Yet after many months of persevering prayers, within a few months of running a small publishing company, a special friend offered me capital to produce more *My Partner Prayer Notebooks.* I was incredibly encouraged that God brought someone else along to believe in and finance the idea He had given me.

After two more years of prayer, numerous rejections, hours of hard work, tons of decisions, and knocking on many doors, we had sold four thousand notebooks. Not long after, a publishing house agreed to publish the notebook (and this book), alleviating many of the production and distribution responsibilities. And the dream rolled on . . . *and is still rolling!*

Prayer is *power waiting to be released!* If believers would only give God their time and love, fear Him, and believe what He says in His Word about prayer, they would find Him *more than willing* to give them the desires of their hearts. Psalm 37:4 declares, "Delight yourself also in the Lord, and He shall give you the desires of your heart" (NKJV). Perhaps the power hidden in that verse is not about your desires, but how you can delight yourself in the Lord?

With the freedom to dream and pray, came a release, as if a waterfall had broken over a dam. More dreams and plans, goals and ideas daily unfolded in my hourly appointments with God—and so did corrections, confessions, and courage. The mounds of miracles only fueled more hope to dream God's dreams, and as I approached each day, He seemed to allow big and little doors to open and close along the way, vividly serving as signs of His direction, goodness, faithfulness, and power.

As always, Scripture entwined with prayer increased my faith to hope and dream and watch for God. Over a four-year period, a powerful example of a dream implanted in my heart by God was realized.

The same friend who had originally loaned the start-up capital for *My Partner Prayer Notebook* had recently attended a large youth congress of the Covenant Church denomination. Upon returning, he and his sister excitedly shared their experiences of spending a week with four thousand kids and the many ways in which God had changed lives. They commented wholeheartedly that a workshop on prayer would have been ideal for a convention of students! With their encouragement, I decided to daily pray and ask God to open doors for me to attend the next CHIC (Covenant High Congress), four years later.

During this time, unbeknownst to me, my name had been suggested to the speakers search committee, and someone was asked to observe one of my speeches while attending a National Youth Workers Convention later that year. Though I knew nothing of these arrangements, I continued daily to ask God for open doors to share about prayer at CHIC.

In February, I overheard a few of my speaker buddies commenting about a summer congress they would be attending—CHIC! Their excitement for the congress—and confirmed speaking dates—startled me into realizing that CHIC was long planned and I was not going to be a part of that particular congress. Disheartened, I almost took CHIC off my prayer list. For some reason I hadn't gotten around to it when I received a phone message in my office mailbox from a person in Massachusetts I had never met but who was from a Covenant Church. As I dialed the phone number, my hand began to shake and my heart leaped with hope that something related to CHIC was developing.

And so it was! Randy, indeed, had called to ask me if I would *consider praying about* being a speaker for CHIC—all the while apologizing for the late notice. I said, "Oh, my goodness, you won't believe this," and I proceeded to tell him of my three-and-a-half-year-long prayer request. Much more than coincidence, God had put a desire in my heart, allowing it to come to pass in such a way as to give Him the glory! Psalm 37:4, "Delight yourself in the Lord, and He will give you the desires of your heart," popped into my heart and mind as reality.

But that was not the end of the excitement of answered prayer. Two years earlier, I had attended a conference, and while listening to a keynote speaker, I was struck with the idea of writing a devotional for students.

From that moment on, the idea would not go away, so I added it to my prayer list *and* began to write the book. I continued to ask God for His ideas and open doors, and though I gained a few people's interest, the manuscript sat in a file drawer. But I never stopped praying about it until I finished writing it.

Two months before CHIC, the high-school convention for thousands students to be held in Colorado, I received a call. "Becky, this is Chuck from CHIC. You may not remember me, but Tic gave me your name. We wondered if you would consider writing a devotional for the high schoolers at CHIC to take home as a follow-up tool? We would need at least four thousand copies." In utter amazement, I told Chuck of my two-year prayer request to write a devotional for high schooler students.

And to pull it all together, someone offered to underwrite the total project and we all witnessed an incredible two-month turnaround of a six-week daily devotional called *Live It.*

Prayer had truly become an adventure of faith. Taking Hebrews 11:6 literally, "Without faith it is impossible to please God," propelled me to have faith in God with the fresh abandon of a dependent child. Wanting even more faith, I found Romans 10:17 to be the interchangeable piece to a two-part puzzle. Prayer and the Word of God were inseparable. *Faith came from hearing His Word.* And the Word exhorted me to pray and call upon God. If tested, as tried and true, prayer and the Word would release incredible power from God into one's life.

PART V
A DEEPER WALK

THE BLESSINGS AND BENEFITS OF PRAYER

Just to pray without ceasing for one hour seemed like a monumental achievement! Yes, amazing answers to prayer elicit whoops and hollers, and persevering prayer teaches endurance, but spending time with Jesus, perhaps as His disciples did—laughing, crying, complaining, proposing, deliberating, submitting, confessing, and praising—became the most wonderful benefit of our daily appointment together.

When prayer became my passion, rather than my duty, I could not stop talking about it. But had you told me that I would spend over two decades speaking and writing about prayer, I would not have believed you! In fact, I don't give a first impression of being a very serious person. And of all the suitable topics someone of my personality could discuss, prayer would—without exception—be the last one chosen by others as the theme of my life.

Perhaps that paradox is the greatest argument I have in my defense when others offer their reasons (or excuses) for not praying. My experience in prayer proves the point that it is not gender, denomination, vocation, or education that causes a person to be an effective pray-er. It is simply one's commitment to spend time with the Lord that makes them powerful in prayer. How one arrives at that decision, whether it is out of crisis, great need, humiliation, or persuasion, seems irrelevant. Priorities, personality, and profession all set aside, it boils down to one question, "Will you make time for God?" When answered with a resounding, "Yes, no matter the cost," then the inevitable results of a deeper walk with God occur *because of prayer.*

Prayer allows God's presence to impact all areas and aspects of one's life, beginning with simple, daily decisions and culminating with one's life purpose. The combination of prayer and the Word takes conjecture out of life and replaces it with certainties. And in the practice of prayer one is escorted farther and deeper into knowing and loving God.

Therefore, imagine one's surprise in stopping after many years of a long journey to reflect on the open doors and detours that took you to place you never imagined when you began. The results of diligent prayer are the highlights of the journey; just to read a list of them is incredibly appealing, but to experience them as personal mile-markers is life-changing!

Throughout the journey of daily prayer and Bible reading I have *experienced and benefited* in six areas of personal and spiritual growth, not because I am in ministry, but because I am a person intent on spending time alone daily with God.

I discovered that…

- Prayer fuels faith to dream and hope and risk.
- Prayer "woos" us to the Word by our need to hear God's response to our requests.
- Prayer teaches trust in God through waiting upon His timing.
- Prayer reveals God's plan and our purpose in opening up to us detailed directions for both the present and the future.
- Prayer releases God's power to live and walk in the supernatural realm of the Holy Spirit.

- Prayer unleashes love for God—emotional, real, and all-consuming.

Who, then, having thought through the benefits of prayer would consciously decide to eliminate, forget, or neglect time with God? Let's walk on . . .

CHAPTER 12

PRAYER FUELS FAITH

Now faith is being sure of what we hope
for and *certain* of what we do not see.
—Hebrews 11:1, emphasis added

How do we receive the peaceful assurance from God that "all things work together for good to those who love God, to those who are the called according to His purpose" (Rom. 8:28, NKJV)? Where does that confidence come from? How can we be sure we are not just chasing after an elusive dream, a "pot of gold," or a rainbow? And when and how does prayer enter into the process of faith—believing in what we expect to happen, but we cannot visibly see?

With the excitement and anticipation of a new building project, an architect and a contractor sit with an owner-buyer, assuring him of successful completion of the project by displaying blueprints, pictures, and sketches of similar completed buildings. They show the owner flowcharts of dates for breaking ground, erecting steel, pouring concrete, and completing the finish work. Though all the components of the building are not even begun, it will eventually be finished and seen by all.

Similarly, time spent with God in conversation regarding one's dreams and hopes puts a form and plan to one's hearts desires, proposing that in God's timing and by His blueprint they will come to pass. Daily discussions with God, the Author and Perfecter of our faith, the Architect of our lives . . .

solidifies details,

develops a calm assurance, and

intensifies one's hope for completion of the "building," providing "brick and mortar" for a previously "vacant lot."

Because an idea or a dream starts in one's heart and mind, believing faith cannot be based on outer circumstances; it must be based on God's inner work of confidence and direction— through His Word and Spirit—which will in turn provide visible "markers" as confirmation along the way.

Yet faith is not passive. It is an action—as is love. To love is

to give,

to accept,

to sacrifice,

to stand with,

to believe in.

To have faith is to step in the direction toward what is believed to be the planned course of our lives. It is obeying God in the unseen areas of our lives. And because it is fueled by God alone, faith cannot develop without prayer and the Word. It is the consecutive string of thoughts, Scriptures, and promptings heard in the inner person, "Keep moving . . . turn here . . . stop briefly . . . knock on this door . . . step quickly," that propels us through the course of a dream, a project, or an idea.

But how can we obey if we haven't heard Him speak? Prayer and the Word

whisper,

call out,

point,
> promise, and
>> lead us in each and every step . . .

if we will only make time to listen.

Faith cannot be mustered up, engineered, or manipulated; it is a response from within us, orchestrated by God. It is a supernatural confidence inspired by a supernatural God.

I often shake my head in awe at the miracle of my conversion to Christ. For six years, from the ages of fifteen to twenty-one, I followed all the "popular" trends: going to wild parties, drinking, dancing, bar hopping, and using drugs. I was caught in a downward spiral—going from a normal, happy, all-American kid to becoming an alcoholic drug addict with suicidal tendencies.

An unusual course of events led me to a small church with one born-again, Spirit-filled janitor on its staff who loved to share the person of Christ with the lost. *Never, in my wildest thoughts, would I have imagined my life turning 180 degrees one hot, sunny, August California afternoon at the invitation of this janitor.*

How did he interest me in changing my entire life when my boyfriend, lifestyle, and goals were so unlike—even opposed to—faith in Christ? He spoke these words: "If anyone is in Christ, he is a new creation; old things have passed away; behold, all things have become new" (2 Cor. 5:17, NKJV). And though this janitor knew of only the brief, sordid details my past and present, he told me that Jesus loved me—just the way I was!

And why, by his suggestion and without struggle or reservation on my part, would I ask Jesus Christ into my heart within minutes of hearing the Good News? Though I could not see ahead, looking back was so painful that the words he spoke offered me hope for a new life. My previous "religious" experiences were not the basis for my newly exhibited, daring faith. Nor had I been able to quit drinking or drugs due to self-determination. No, *I was without hope* for healing, no money even for outpatient recovery. I had literally depleted any reservoir of self-respect. What could cause such a turnaround?

I believe the first step of faith took place when I believed what that janitor said about his Jesus: (1) He did and would always love me, and (2) He was going to make my life new.

The second step occurred when I repeated the "sinner's prayer," begging Jesus to come into my heart and forgive me of my many sins and make me new. I walked away from that time in prayer convinced I was an immediately transformed person! There is no other explanation for the instant removal of the compelling and overwhelming thoughts that lured me to drink or how the physical craving for alcohol had been removed, never to return. In that moment of prayer, I was miraculously released from the bondage alcohol and drugs had upon me. Equally drastic changes in my lifestyle, friends, and habits were just the initial "wave" of new life in Christ!

Almost immediately, strange and "unusual" cravings developed within me. In only hours after my conversion, I began . . .

> to read the Bible,
>> to pray, and
>>> to tell others about Jesus.

To say I was a "sinner" saved would be stating the depth of my depravity mildly. Yet the question remained: How could I have changed so abruptly and dramatically?

I can only attribute the accelerated changes in a few short months . . .

> from alcoholic to evangelist,
> from "worldly" to spiritual,
> from a foul mouth to a clean mouth,
> from immoral to moral,

from habitual liar to truth-teller,
from worrier to pray-er,
from irreligious to incessant Bible reader . . .
to a faith *supernaturally implanted within me* to believe in the
living Christ and His Word. The moment I dared to believe
that Jesus could and would change my life from old to new—
though I could not see how—and chose to believe God's Word
as literal, I was rescued, delivered, and saved through faith in
the Son of God.

Less than one month after my born-again experience, a
small group of Christians laid hands on a completely sober and
"straight" twenty-one-year-old and prayed a seemingly unusual
prayer. They prayed for God's Holy Spirit to empower me as an
evangelist—*throughout the world.* Strange, don't you think? I
had barely escaped the fires of hell, and they had me gallivanting across the world sharing about Jesus! It would be months
later before I would read I Timothy 4:14: "Do not neglect
your gift, which was given you through a prophetic message
when the body of elders laid their hands on you."

Not knowledgeable regarding Christian organizations or
the church, a few months later, I returned to my parents'
hometown and within a year was on staff with a local Youth
for Christ chapter. Over the past thirty years I have shared my
testimony in books, on radio, and on television throughout the
United States and in other countries.

Could I ever have imagined that, in the first months after
my conversion to Christ, God would have such a detailed and
dynamic plan for one who was so lost and undeserving of any
kindness? No. But *faith is believing what you cannot see.* It is
taking a step toward where you believe God is leading. It is not
looking back. It is not rationalizing. It is not reasoning. It is
daring to believe that the God of the universe can direct one's
life; that He is able and willing . . .

to intervene if we'll call on Him,
to bring the spiritually "dead" to life,
to bring healing and health to the sick, and
to give hope for tomorrow—no matter how
bleak tomorrow looks.

Like the architect needs a builder, prayer and faith combine together to direct and complete us. Prayer is our appointment with God. Faith is our exhibition of trust and willingness in follow His plan for our lives. Hebrews 11:6 challenges, "Without faith it is impossible to please God."

CHAPTER 13

PRAYER WOOS TO THE WORD

Meant to sustain, inspire, motivate, increase faith, mature, and strengthen a believer, the Word of God, when interwoven with prayer, serves as direction and guidance, conviction and comfort, a deterrent from sin, an escape, a counselor. A deeper walk with Christ is evident when our *first* response, our most compelling desire at any given time, in any situation, is to hunger for the advice found in God's Word.

Theophan, known as the Recluse, said if they were practiced simultaneously, the Word and prayer produced a certain feeling within the believer toward the Lord:

> *Do you wish to enter this Paradise as quickly as possible? Here, then, is what you must do. When you pray, do not end your prayer without having aroused in your heart some feeling toward God, whether it be reverence, or devotion, or thanksgiving, or glorification, or humility and contrition, or hope and trust. Also when after prayer you begin to read, do not finish reading without having felt in your heart the truth of what you read. These two feelings—the one inspired by prayer, the other by reading—mutually*

warm one another; and if you pay attention to your-
self, they will keep you under their influence during
the whole day. Take pains to practice these two meth-
ods exactly and you will see for yourself what will
happen.

What *will* happen? He continues, "God's spark, the ray of
grace will fall at last into your heart. There is no way in which
you, yourself, can produce it: it comes forth direct from God."

Recently, on an early evening flight home after an all-day
seminar, I sank into my aisle seat, and out of pure exhaustion
I stuffed my carry-on bags under the seat in front of me and
sighed with relief at the sight of an empty row next to me.
Tired, yet keenly aware of the deadline of another project beck-
oning for my attention, I closed my eyes and wondered if I had
enough energy to keep working. In that brief moment of silence, a thought crossed my mind: *You haven't read your Bible*
yet today. And the words following that thought were these:
Becky, if you open your Bible, I'll speak to you. I smiled and sighed
with a deep contentment. I prayed, "Oh, You know I need You
right now. I'm stretched beyond what I can do. You are here
with me, and through Your Word, You want to speak to me."

I reached down and pulled out my Bible, *expecting* to hear
from my Lord. What I got was more than I had anticipated.
While reading in the book of Joshua, I ran across these words:
"Choose for yourselves this day whom you will serve. . . . as for
me and my household, we will serve the Lord" (24:15).

I closed my eyes, just to reflect on the timing of God's
Word—on a plane, after a long day of co-leading a Resource
Seminar for Youth Workers, in my heart I felt the Lord's ac-
knowledgment of my service. Ironically, I had been listening to
music through earphones, and the song "Angels Watching
Over Me" began to play. I laughed, thinking: *Here I am, up in*

the sky, with the angels, having just served God, praying for encouragement and motivation, and I can smile as these words and circumstances are falling together in this way.

Then, the plane tipped just a bit, and a warm, bright ray of sunshine filled my empty row and rested on my face. I kept my eyes closed, wanting to soak in as much of God as I could in this moment. The light turned from bright yellow to orange and then to a deep red as I kept my eyes closed. Quietly, I felt I heard God's voice whisper, "Hi!" His voice seemed so casual, so relaxed. So I responded in my thoughts with, *Hi!* I couldn't help but smile. I knew at that point I could let myself discount this encounter or I could just let it flow. I decided to "go for it." The next words I heard were, "I love you." Without skipping a beat, I said, *I love You, too.* Then I felt as if God said, "I know." Tears warmed my cheeks. Our conversation continued for a few minutes. Then as the warmth of the sun withdrew, I looked down at my Bible resting upon my lap. What if I hadn't opened my Bible?

Prayer draws us to the Word, and the two ignite to create a spark, even a flame in our hearts for the Lord. The Word and prayer, if *applied* to all circumstances of our lives, are *intended* to change, transform, motivate, and propel us to make certain decisions, take deliberate steps, and stretch us to live and walk in the Spirit. But until Bible reading and prayer become our *natural* reaction when faced with a dilemma or a decision, we'll not experience the warmth described by Theophan—the spark that allows God to confirm direction or grant peace amidst turmoil. If prayer is simply a last resort "call for help" and if we only haphazardly searches the Scriptures for guidance (when all other avenues have failed), we have missed God's true intent of how prayer and the Word are able to integrate moment by moment into a believer's life.

Though I've experienced countless situations where God's Word affected my directions and responses, one such time I'll always remember happened while speaking at a retreat. A negative and hurtful miscommunication occurred. Because we were all Christians, I optimistically confronted the situation, speaking the truth in love, but was thoroughly heartbroken over the rejections that followed.

In my hotel room, I prayed, cried, and spoke to my roommate. Frustrated, I opened the Bible, but disappointment and anger kept me from finding comfort in the Word. I proceeded to roll over and turn off the light. Sensing my distress, my roommate made a suggestion, but something didn't seem "right." But what was right?

It was then that I knew what was left for me to do. This was a very sensitive situation. I had to be still and look to God (not my friends or my feelings) to show me exactly what to do. Therefore, I decided to get up early the next morning to have my quiet time, search the Word for God's counsel, and fully express myself to Him, confessing any sin and/or anger on my part. Then before confronting the issue any further, I would call my husband and relay the situation, share my findings, and seek any additional counsel, especially because I was so emotional over the whole episode.

Beginning each morning's quiet time in the book of Psalms, I should not have been surprised that the words of the next few chapters were . . .

"deliver me . . .

rescue me . . .

be my shield and my refuge . . . "

In searching my heart and motives amidst this awkward situation of broken promises and in light of the morning Scripture passages, I felt God was on my side. I called my husband and shared my concerns. I found him compassionate, but received a strong warning from him to handle the issue gently, letting God deal with the broken pieces. During the last day of the retreat, when the outer circumstances did not change, I fought to hold on to my personal integrity though I was tempted to get angry. My only consolation was God's word to me of His faithfulness and promised deliverance.

It was at least six months later when the woman from the retreat, forty years older than me, called unexpectedly one morning. She said, "Becky, I feel God spoke to me this morning and told me to call you and apologize for what happened at the retreat last year." Almost speechless, because I never thought I would hear from her again, I quietly acknowledged her apology.

The comfort of God's Word, in the midst of uncontrollable circumstances brought His strength and promise into my hurting heart during the retreat. He knew much more time would be needed to reconcile the relationship. The warmth of God's Word and much prayer became my only resources for "pressing on" during those silent months until His work was complete.

A deeper walk with God emerges when the Word is constantly *blended* with prayer in a believer's life. David mentions several times in Psalm 119 that he put his hope in the Word. Because of that exhortation, it has become my practice to hope in the Word by asking God for scriptural promises to hold on to or to "hope in" when my endurance level is waning or when I have a long wait or big decision to make. It is as if He gives a promise—His promise—to be my visible possession while waiting for the invisible to happen. My Bible, especially the books of Isaiah and Psalms, is splashed with underlined verses, highlighted paragraphs, and dated ink marks next to verses that were my hope while waiting for difficult situations to resolve or for a broken relationship to be mended. God's Word, whether read during my quiet time or heard during timely sermon texts, encouraged me when I needed a lift, guided me *before* making purchases or accepting invitations.

Seeing verse 46 of Psalm 119 underlined and dated March 1, 1988 reminds me of God's promise when I really needed Him: "I will speak of your statutes before kings and will not be put to shame." For example, the week before I was to share my testimony (of being a teenage alcoholic) in an Ohio public high school, I was told the principal was unsure that I would be able to handle all the students because I was a woman. That didn't do much for building my confidence, so I opened the Word and asked God to speak to me, to confirm His call upon my life, to assure me that He would be with me—even to go ahead of me. That morning's *Change Your Life Daily Bible* reading in the book of Psalms had me in chapter 119 where God was able to say, "You'll not be put to shame." One week before I had to be at that high school, God's words could not have been more timely or comforting!

The verses that are marked in my Bible remind me of how God encouraged me to trust Him during personal and difficult situations and circumstances. They gave me great hope on a specific day, though someone else might have overlooked those very verses. That is why it is so important to have a regular, daily Bible reading plan, so you personally grow familiar with God's Word *as His voice*. Then you can run to His promises with the fresh abandon of children, reaching for your Father's hand to catch you before a fall or just to feel His warm, firm grip when you're insecure or afraid.

Daily Bible reading, along with prayer, encourages a two-way conversation with God, allowing the warmth of the right direction to overpower the dullness or confusion that accompanies wrong or incorrect choices.

In *The Inner Life*, Andrew Murray proposes . . .

> *Prayer and the Word are inseparably linked together.*
> *Power in the use of either depends upon the presence*
> *of the other. The Word gives me guidance for prayer,*
> *telling me what God will do for me. It shows me the*
> *path of prayer, telling me how God would have me*
> *come. It gives me the power for prayer, the courage to*
> *accept the assurance that I will be heard. And it*
> *brings me the answer to prayer, as it teaches what*
> *God will do for me. And so, prayer prepares the heart*
> *for receiving the Word from God Himself, for the*
> *teaching of the Spirit which gives spiritual under-*
> *standing, and for the faith that carries out God's*
> *will.*

It takes a *time commitment* and *daily practice* to walk deeper into knowing God through the utterly available combination of the Word and prayer. When opening the Bible and talking to God in prayer become...

our *first* option,

our *natural* instinct,

our *immediate* reaction when faced with a decision or problem, then we will have a deep assurance that we are walking hand in hand along the pathway of our earthly lives with our Lord and Friend.

CHAPTER 14

PRAYER TEACHES TRUST IN GOD'S TIMING

> Suppose a man made me a hundred promises.
> And he had ten years to fulfill them. In the next
> month the ten years would expire. He has ful-
> filled 99 of the promises and he is able to fulfill
> the other. Would not I have good reason to
> trust him that he would fulfill it?
> —D. L. Moody

A pattern develops when we pray for a specific request for days and weeks and even years . . .

First pray . . .

then wait. . .

then receive.

How we wait upon God's timing says a lot about the depth of our trust in God.

Luis Palau suggests that Saul's "damaging dead end" as king of Israel resulted from his impatient, nervous restlessness . . . his running ahead of God, not waiting for God's signals. Oh, how often do those words classify our own personalities in prayer?

The discipline of daily prayer teaches us to wait or trust in God's best. Over the course of our prayer journeys (as we've discussed in previous chapters), we'll discover that much of what we ask God for is His will, but the timing is wrong! It is only later, when all the pieces slip neatly into place that we can ponder and appreciate the extra benefits of what "time and waiting" allowed to transpire.

Accounts in biographies of George Muller, Hudson Taylor, Jim Elliot, Charles Finney, and Peter and Catherine Marshall detail tremendous stories of waiting and trusting and persevering in prayer, for years in many cases, before the answer to a specific prayer request was revealed by God. And so it is in the life of any believer who prays *without giving up*. Accounts of healing, a job opening, a miraculous serendipity in meeting someone special, a financial blessing, or a long-awaited dream fulfilled at last are the results of waiting!

Though we may not receive the answer to our prayers we envisioned, our attitude in prayer is to never stop waiting, trusting, praying, or expecting God to do "immeasurably more than all we could ask or imagine" in answer to our request. And what do we find out about God at the end of a long-term wait? O. Hallesby declares, "When He grants our prayers, it is because He loves us. When He does not, it is also because He loves us." We are to trust Him because He loves us.

But be warned! Understanding the dynamics of persevering prayer comes only from the actual *experience* of praying. Phrases, comments, and clichés about prayer sound so inspirational, perhaps even motivational. But only through truly waiting upon God and His response to a prayer request can one develop an inner trust in God that is *sure* of His provision, though the details are unseen.

Patience and perseverance in prayer come not from begging God, but from waiting on Him. The discipline of waiting includes asking God if we are praying rightly, if we've heard His promise accurately. It involves evaluating our motives, honestly examining if they are impure or selfish, and being able to acknowledge when our hopes are centered on something other than God's will.

Perseverance in prayer includes a willingness to let Him alter or change our requests in prayer according to His plan. And especially over an extended time of seeming silence, we who wait on God must be careful that our persistence in prayer does not become anxiety that saps strength; rather, it should be anticipation of His will that increases the endurance to persevere. Again, O. Hallesby captures the timing of prayer: "The more completely you cease being concerned about the TIME in which your prayers are to be answered, the more freedom you'll enjoy in your prayer life!"

CHAPTER 15

PRAYER REVEALS GOD'S PLAN AND OUR PURPOSE

James 1:5 says, "If any of you lacks wisdom, he should ask God, who gives generously to all without finding fault, and it will be given to him." I believe that God's Word means what it says. If God says it is okay to ask Him for wisdom to make decisions or plans, it would demean this Scripture if I wondered and worried about whether God wanted to show me His will. I'd emotionally be a mess, "driven and tossed by the wind," as James continues to warn the person who doubts once God has shown him His answers. The Word gives one the complete confidence that if and when one asks, God will answer!

First John 5:14-15 reiterates that verse by stating, "This is the confidence we have in approaching God: that if we ask anything according to his will, he hears us. And if we know that he hears us—whatever we ask—we know that we have what we asked of him."

Sometimes God's Word is so loud and clear that we're afraid or intimidated by its directives, especially when it comes to asking, hearing, knowing, and doing His will. We get tripped up by the timing of the answer or by people around us who may negatively influence us or by a fear of looking foolish. That's when looking at the Word for real-life illustrations of those who sought God's specific plan—and received it—provides encouragement to believe that the principle is the same for anyone who loves God and fears Him.

What would Israel have been like without the prayers and obedience of Joseph, Moses, Daniel, and Samuel asking and receiving God's specific direction for travel, battle, rations, words of knowledge, and strength? And why would we in our life's journey of battles, travels, and physical needs be any less needy of God's specific direction?

Granted, there are a few "minor" prerequisites for knowing God's will, as the psalmist mentions in Psalm 25:12, "Who, then, is the man that fears the Lord? He will instruct him in the way chosen for him." And he continues, "The Lord confides in those who fear him; he makes his covenant known to them" (v. 14).

I am convinced by Scripture and personal experience that "fearing" God—loving, revering, and obeying Him—is the pathway to asking for and obtaining God's will for one's life. From one's personal relationship with God, one gains the assurance that He indeed has a specific plan for one's life. Then as Matthew 21:22 says, "If you believe [in what He has shown you is the way to pray . . . His will], you will receive whatever you ask for in prayer."

In the large and small circumstances, in the lives of the weak and strong, for the famous and infamous, God has a plan. Psalm 139:16 points to that truth:

> *All the days ordained for me were written in your*
> *book before one of them came to be.*

May I be so bold to say that *when* I have asked, I have always received my "marching orders," and because God has shown me the way, I know where I am going. I have received a call, and I'm following.

Ask for His will,
  believe in what God says is yours, until you
  receive all that He has for you.

In the book *Guide to Prayer for Ministers and Other Servants* is an excerpt from *The Art of Prayer*, which offers a beautiful description of asking, receiving, and even writing down prayers:

> You write that at times, during prayer, a solution to some problem that perplexes you in your spiritual life comes out of itself from an unknown source. This is good. It is the true Christian way of being taught God's truth. Here the promise is fulfilled and they shall be taught of God (John 6:45). So indeed it is. Truths are inscribed in the heart by the finger of God and remain there firm and indelible. Do not neglect these truths which God inscribes but write them down. And upon writing down the direction one believes God is taking them and acting upon what is written down I have no doubt or reservation to say one will know God's will for their lives.

The book of Proverbs is full of sage advice, not the least of which is this: "In all your ways, acknowledge Him, and He shall direct your paths" (3:6, NKJV). Which of us would not want to have the directions to the very best of all possible plans made available? A habit of inquiring of God in all situations will inevitably—as promised—reveal His plans.

CHAPTER 16

PRAYER RELEASES GOD'S POWER

Prayer releases God's power
. . . in the life of a person.
. . . in the life of a church.
. . . in the life of a community.
. . . in the life of a country.

Has not prayer been the means used to escort a sinner through the gates of salvation into eternal life? Has not prayer been the vehicle that ushers in the Holy Spirit's power to bring about physical healing and to turn one man—even a convict—from the depths of sin and ungodliness (whether it be the apostle Paul or a David Wilkerson) into an itinerant evangelist? Does not prayer precede miracles of inner healing? Is not concerted prayer the groundwork for revival?

In the New International Version of the Bible, James 5:16 reads, "The prayer of a righteous man is powerful and effective," and in the New King James Version it is stated, "The effective, fervent prayer of a righteous man avails much." If prayer had no power or even little power, what would be its purpose? Since prayer is presented as an effective *source of power* for the believer, it appears unwise, even foolish, to approach life without it—at least as foolish as it would be to go into enemy territory without weapons for defense.

Could it be that we neglect prayer because we don't have a *need* for power in our daily lives? I doubt that. I know not one life that has no struggle or disappointment, does not face some opposition or illness, has not experienced pain or tragedy to some degree, and therefore has no need for God's power to be released.

So, to whom is the power available, and how does prayer release God's power? Forgive me if my answer seems simple, but I am convinced the source of God's power to change, re-arrange, create, move, and transform a believer's life is the person of the Holy Spirit.

I say this not because I am an expert on the subject, but because I have experienced and witnessed supernatural power and intervention in countless circumstances where, through an invitation to the Holy Spirit in prayer, God's power was released to avail much! Through reading books such as *The Helper* by Catherine Marshall and having been led to Christ by an enthusiastic, charismatic Christian, I have been open to and intrigued by the Holy Spirit of God. All the while, though, I've observed many people who are intimidated by the same powerful Holy Spirit, avoiding and essentially ignoring Him and His available power.

For whatever reason—misunderstanding, fear, or doubt—when the Holy Spirit is not invited by believers into their lives or circumstances, it appears they have pulled the plug to their power source—God Himself.

Not only is the book of Acts an incredible account of the works and power of the Holy Spirit, but Jesus Himself implored His disciples to wait upon and cling to His Holy Spirit. Jesus promised that His Spirit would *empower* them (Acts 1:8) and teach them truth and provide counsel. He would take what was His and make it *known* to them (John 15—16)! Paul prayed for the Ephesians: "I pray that out of his [God's] glorious riches he may strengthen you with power through his Spirit in your inner being, so that Christ may dwell in your heart through faith" (Eph. 3:16-17).

I am not naive enough to assume that my few words of testimony and Scripture regarding the power released when one invites the person of the Holy Spirit into one's life or circumstances will dramatically convince or change one's thoughts or beliefs in this area. But I am willing to challenge anyone who will be open to leaving the supernatural releasing of power up to God! To do this, pray daily (at the start of each new day and after a regular time of confession) this simple prayer:

> Lord, fill me up to overflowing with Your Holy Spirit this day. I commit my ways to You.

Then wait in anticipation for God's power to be released within your life in (perhaps) both unusual and supernatural ways.

Jesus said, "If you then, though you are evil, know how to give good gifts to your children, how much more will your Father in heaven give the Holy Spirit to those who ask him!" (Luke 11:13).

CHAPTER 17

PRAYER UNLEASHES LOVE FOR GOD

Andrew Murray asked, "What is it that makes the inner chamber so powerless?" And he answered his own question by saying, "The world's fellowship is more attractive than being alone with the Heavenly Father."

All the words and sentences in this book have urged each of us to look at our relationship with God through prayer.

Is prayer the intimate time with God that is in creasing as we pass through daily experiences?

Is prayer the confidential conversations we have with our Best Friend?

Is prayer an expression of our commitment to God?

For some of us, if it is, we're in trouble.

Should our love relationship with God be considered any differently from our other relationships? If we, for whatever reason, neglect to spend time with Him, is that love? I have found no better challenge that I could leave you with than this from *The God Who Comes* by Carlo Carretto:

> If a fiancé telephones his fiancée to tell her, "I'm sorry, this evening I can't come, I've so much work!", there is nothing wrong. But if it is the

thousandth time he has made the same call, he has not been to see her in week on the excuse of work outings with friends, it is more serious—rather, it is quite clear: this is not love. . . .

If you don't pray, if you are not searching for a personal relationship with God, if you don't stay with him for long periods in order to know him, study him, understand him, little by little you will start forgetting him, your memory will weaken, you will no longer recognize him. You will not be able to, because you will no longer know how to love.

. . . Have you
  been not praying,
    not seeking him personally
      because you don't love him or
        because you have no time?

My purpose in writing this book is to motivate and inspire every reader to plan on and look forward to spending time with God. In the prayer workshops and seminars that I conduct, I would feel negligent if I just "told a good story," but did not challenge the people to evaluate their present prayer lives and then make a practical decision in relationship to spending time with the Lord. Therefore, if you've not already made prayer a daily part of your life, and you feel compelled by God's Holy Spirit to make such a commitment of your time and love, I would ask you to join me in the following prayer:

O Lord, I believe that You have a personal plan for my life that will affect the world around me for You if I will daily spend time with You in prayer and diligently look for You and listen to You through Your Word and Spirit. Cause me to meet with You every day in a regular appointment for the rest of my life. Fill me with Your Holy Spirit, woo me to Your Word, increase my faith, and develop within me an incredible love for You. I ask these things in Jesus' name. Amen.

THE POWER
OF FASTING

The Next Step

In 1984, I began the journey of becoming a woman who prays daily. Through a simple life-changing decision, I took a huge leap from praying little to praying much. Over fifteen years, one day and one hour a time, I have developed a deep passion for prayer.

Because I am not a serious, quiet, or studious person, the mere fact that I have been able to quiet my heart and mind for sixty minutes each day has been quite a stretching experience, and yet it only prepared me for something more.

Five years after I first wrote *Let Prayer Change Your Life*, in May of 1995, I was challenged by Dr. Bill Bright of Campus Crusade for Christ. He presented the spiritual discipline of fasting by sharing his experience and issued a call to fasting.

Discovering the Discipline of Fasting

I confess that I knew little about fasting. So I decided to read his book *The Coming Revival: A Call to Fasting and*

Prayer. With much fear and reservation, I got on a plane and finished reading the book before we even landed.

In his book, Dr. Bright called each reader to consider being one of two million believers in North America who would fast forty days, for revival in America, before the end of the year 2000. He believed that with fasting *and* prayer our country would turn back to living for and loving the God of the Bible.

His book describes what can happen if a person will fast and gives practical suggestions on *how* to fast, as well as the biblical principles behind fasting. It is designed to encourage you to fast, whether you commit to one day or forty. Note: In addition to the above-mentioned book, Bright's booklet *Seven Basic Steps to Fasting* encourages consultation with a doctor before partaking of a fast.)

Just as I had unexpectedly uncovered the powerful principles about prayer through a workshop years ago, through Dr. Bright's influence and impassioned challenge I discovered and committed to the spiritual discipline of fasting.

Deciding to Fast

Shortly after reading the book, I followed Dr. Bright's suggestion to lay out a plan to partake of a forty-day "partial" fast, rather than to attempt a "complete" fast. (Note: A "complete" fast would mean drinking only water and abstaining from all food products, including juices. A "partial" fast includes abstinence from certain foods or all foods, but not from liquid juices or broths.) For my first forty-day "partial" fast, I decided that I would fast from all food for ten days and drink only juices. The next twenty days I would drink juices until dinnertime then have a dinner each night of fruit and vegetables only. The remaining ten days of my fast included three meals of fruit, vegetables, and grains.

Designing a Fast

My fast followed many of the guidelines found in Dr. Bright's book:

1. I limited my exercise during those forty days.
2. I chose a forty-day period when I did not have a heavy travel schedule or workload.
3. I purchased a juicer, in order to drink nonacid juices during my days of all-liquid fasting.

I defined a threefold purpose for fasting. In addition to praying for revival in America, I asked God to show me what part I ought to play in the coming revival. And third, I prayed for break through in my teenage son's life. During this period of fasting, my entire prayer time became more intense as I also prayed more diligently for those who had specific and sometimes desperate needs and concerns.

Within the first six days of the fast, I experienced a definite breakthrough. First, a friend for whom I had prayed for daily and who had been unemployed for more than a year got a job. Midway though the fast an exciting opportunity opened up for me to expand my work of speaking and writing. And by the end of the fast, my teenage son's life appeared to take a detour, but quickly made a turn back toward "home."

Almost every day of the fast, my own heart and mind were being broken and humbled to see areas of my life that needed to change. I attributed each of these breakthroughs to the powerful combination of fasting *and* prayer.

Just as prayer had transformed every area of my life, the results of my first fast had an impact on every area of my life—physically, emotionally, and spiritually.

Physically

I thought that it was appropriate that I not confuse my motives during this fast, so I did not weigh myself before or after the fast. And though I did seem to lose some body fat, my calorie intake of juices was enough to keep me from becoming too lean! While abstaining from food, I was surprised to find how important and pleasurable food really was to me. Because I was not eating, I realized how often I wanted to eat (1) simply for emotional comfort, (2) to better enjoy a social gathering, or (3) just to satisfy certain cravings.

Without eating for pleasure or comfort, I became very aware of how dependent I had become on food for emotional satisfaction, rather than as nutritional fuel for my body! Fortunately, as time went on, I experienced a complete disinterest, even a dislike, for certain foods such as meat, cheese, and sweets, none of which were included in my fast.

I can honestly say that my body and mind affectionately fought over food for forty days!

Emotionally and Spiritually

My first fast was motivating in every sense. I found within myself a reserve of willpower that I didn't know existed. Later, I would come to under stand that it was probably more of a supernatural power than my own strength giving me courage to abstain from the food that I loved, enjoyed, and missed. I believe this was the power of the Holy Spirit helping to override my mind and body's desire for food, helping me to do something that was not easy to do and for benefits that I might only later experience. I was definitely motivated to continue the discipline of fasting in my life because I saw breakthrough in areas where prayer alone had not resulted in a change.

Upon completing my first "partial" fast, I sensed I was embarking on an exciting spiritual adventure, and I wanted to learn more. Thus, I soaked up every book that I could find about fasting. I was not surprised to find that most of the authors were dead, but their words were fully alive with practical instruction, unwavering passion, and persuasive motivation for why a person should fast.

Just as I was convinced that prayer could change my life, I became convinced that regular fasting was another discipline that could deepen my relationship with God and bring about significant change in my life, and even the world.

Continuing the Discipline

Because of the positive changes I saw in my son's life during my first fast, I concluded that I should continue to fast once a week (sometimes one meal and often for twenty-four hours) for him throughout his high school and college years.

It has been a joy to watch my son graduate from college and follow his heart and call into mission work and teaching. I observed interesting conversations and breakthroughs that often occurred immediately following these times of fasting and prayer for him. Because of this, I continue to pray and fast for him regularly, believing that every parent has a true responsibility and privilege to spiritually care for their child all of their lives.

I have also continued praying and fasting for revival in America, always asking God to show me what my part should be. Though in the beginning, the discipline of fasting seemed overwhelming, by having a plan, I have been able to fast hundreds of meals, asking God to break through in my life and the world. I share this with you to serve as both an encouragement and an illustration! Even with a busy travel and work schedule, a spouse and child, and other commitments, you can incorporate the spiritual discipline of fasting into your life.

Like prayer, I have found that the spiritual discipline of fasting has caused me to know God better and has deepened my desire to make Him known.

Here is what stood out to me after much research on the subject of fasting, I have concluded that:

1. Fasting is a spiritual discipline that not only Jesus spoke about and modeled (Mark 9:29; Matt. 4:2f), but also Old Testament figures practiced in order to see breakthrough in their lives and for their countries (e.g., Esther, Jehoshaphat, Ezra, Nehemiah, etc.).

2. Fasting involves a fresh humbling and submission of oneself unto God with results that are not always expected and do not always remain private!

It has now been more than a decade since I added the discipline of fasting to my life. God has called me to two forty-day and two thirty-day partial fasts during that time, as well as many shorter and more spontaneous fasts for special purposes. During the past four years, I have kept a fasting journal in addition to my prayer journal.

By October 23, 1998, I completed my fortieth day of twenty-four-hour fasts for revival in America! And in 1999, I made a decision to fast another forty days for revival in America before the end of the year 2000. *On the last Friday of the year 2000,* I had an opportunity to share my testimony in a short five minute interview on the CBS Early Show for 2.5 million people! I consider it no coincidence that I had prayed and fasted for revival in America for over five years and on December 29, 2000, I was able to share a life-changing story with more people in five minutes than as a speaker for almost two decades!

But the impact of praying and fasting for revival didn't end there!

By October 2004, continually impacted by Dr. Bill Bright's passion for revival, I founded a student ministry called, Burning Hearts, Inc. It is based on the 1947 Fellowship of the Burning Hearts that Bill Bright, Henrietta Mears, Richard Halverson, and Louis Evans, Jr. began as a "revival cry" to college students of their era. The focus of Burning Hearts, Inc. is simply to call *this* generation of students to return to revival—to be sold out to prayer, set apart in purity, and sent out with purpose (www.theburningheartcontract.com).

By December of 2005, I asked students and campus ministers across America to join me for 40 Days of Prayer for Revival on College Campuses—and they responded! Beginning January 20, 2006 and ending on March 1, 2006, students at private, state and Christian schools held 24 hour prayer vigils on their campuses! For forty consecutive days, I visited each "prayer room" and watched God's Spirit move. All the results aren't in yet, but the prayers of students released powerful change in individuals, and momentum and passion broke loose on campuses across this country. Most importantly, a passion for prayer continues to sweep this nation's students—they are desperate for more of God and praying for a sweeping revival to take hold in our country!

I hope my brief testimony encourages you to take action:

1. Consider fasting and praying for revival in America until you see it.
2. Gather up all of the resources you can find regarding fasting for spiritual breakthrough and read them with an open heart and mind.

3. Pray about the kind of fast God would have you undertake. Fasting does not always mean abstinence from food; it could include abstaining from television, certain foods, etc.

Fasting is not confined to abstinence from eating and drinking. Fasting really means voluntary abstinence for a specified time from the various necessities of life, such as food, drink, sleep, rest, association with people and so forth. "The purpose . . . is to loosen to some degree the ties which bind us to the world of material things and our surroundings as a whole, in order that we may concentrate all our spiritual powers upon the unseen and eternal things." (O. Hallesby, *Prayer*, 114)

4. Decide to fast and pray for specific breakthrough for yourself and others. I strongly recommend fasting if you: (a) have come to an impasse in a situation, (b) have not been able to overcome a weakness, (c) are desperate for an answer, or (d) need special wisdom in a specific situation.

Many of the books I have read on the spiritual discipline of fasting cautioned that a one-meal, one-day, or a onetime fast does not guarantee that a change will occur in a situation any more than a one-minute prayer might be considered an effective way to bring about a significant change. I have found that fasting, if done with a prayerful purpose, over time, *will* result in change and breakthrough.

If you decide to fast, make sure you make the following preparations:

Detail a fasting plan on your calendar. If you schedule your fasting times—in writing—in advance, you will be more apt to follow through with the plan, rather than being caught off guard by unexpected appointments or forgetfulness.

Define your purpose for fasting in a fasting and prayer journal. Make these purposes the focus of your prayer time during the fast. Write them down in a journal and record and date any break throughs or changes. These journal entries will give you motivation to proceed when your endurance levels get low.

Prepare yourself physically. Consult a doctor before beginning a "partial" or "complete" fast. Expect that your energy levels will be lower than normal; therefore, do not maintain a rigorous exercise schedule during a fast. A daily walking plan might be the best way to increase your energy level without exhausting yourself physically.

Prepare yourself emotionally and spiritually. A time of transparent, honest confession (to God and to others) prior to any fast is essential for having a clean and ready heart, mind, and spirit. Unforgiveness, unresolved issues, or unconfessed sin will hinder answered prayer and any breakthrough that would otherwise result from fasting.

Be accountable to another person. It is often easier to fast when others know that you are fasting or especially when they are fasting along with you.

Expect breakthrough and opposition. Whenever a believer desires to grow, change, seek more of God, or do something great for God, there will be not only discouraging setbacks, but incredible interventions. Daily time spent reading and studying the Word of God will result in increased faith and endurance during the "up and down" times that occur during every fast. You will be given courage and strength to sustain you during a fast as you uncover in God's Word how others persevered, attempted great things, and believed what they could not see.

A Final Challenge . . .

I used to think that prayer was boring and that fasting was for monks. Since discovering the power of fasting and prayer, I've determined to make these two disciplines a regular part of my life. I am now personally convinced that fasting, in addition to prayer, increases several godly characteristics:

- A listening and sensitive spirit
- A humbled heart and attitude
- A willingness to make temporary sacrifices for a more permanent cause or outcome
- An extra measure of inner discipline that prompts increased outer discipline
- Awareness of an unseen world where spiritual powers are at war
- An eagerness and urgency that does not wane in the waiting
- A determination that is sustainable
- A willingness to follow through on steps of obedience, even though they may be uncomfortable or uneasy.

It is my hope that you will want to learn more about fasting by prayerfully asking God what He would have you do with this spiritual discipline.

About the Author

Becky Tirabassi is founder and president of the multi-media corporation, Becky Tirabassi Change Your Life, Inc.®, as well as the founder of a non-profit student ministry, Burning Hearts, Inc.

For more information on Change Your Life® events, media appearances, or to order *Let Prayer Change Your Life Workbook*, the *Change Your Life Daily Bible*, *My Partner Prayer Notebook* and other resources:

Write, call, e-mail, or log onto . . .

Becky Tirabassi Change Your Life®, Inc.
Box 9672
Newport Beach, CA 92660
1-800-444-6189
tlc@changeyourlifedaily.com
www.changeyourlifedaily.com

For information on student resources, meetings, or to send tax deductible donations to Burning Hearts, Inc., contact:

Burning Hearts, Inc.
Box 10926
Newport Beach, Ca. 92658
www.theburningheartcontract.com
letters@theburningheartcontract.com

ORDER FORM

		QTY	AMT
My Partner Prayer Notebook	$ 30.00 X _____	=	_____
My Partner Refills	$ 10.00 X _____	=	_____
Let Prayer Change Your Life	$ 13.00 X _____	=	_____
Let Prayer CYL Workbook	$ 25.00 X _____	=	_____
Let Prayer DVD Leaders Kit	$110.00 X _____	=	_____
Let Prayer DVD Event Series	$ 60.00 X _____	=	_____
Change Your Life Daily Bible	$ 20.00 X _____	=	_____

SUBTOTAL $ _____

TAX (CA. RESIDENTS .0775 x SUB) + _____

_____

SUBTOTAL $ _____

SHIPPING ($3.00 x ____ # of BOOKS= _____) + _____

HANDLING (\$2/ORDER) + $ 2

TOTAL (Subtotal + Shpg + Hdl + Tax) $ _____

Send form with check or credit card info to:
BTCYL, Inc., Box 9672, Newport Beach, Ca. 92660

CC # _____   _____ **exp** _____

V code (3 digits on back of card) _____

Signature _____